Haunted Britain:

The Ultimate Paranormal Tourist's UK Handbook

By Lee Brickley

Introduction

The UK is home to some of the most haunted places in the world, and it has a long and fascinating history of ghostly encounters and paranormal activity. For those who are interested in the supernatural, there's no better place to visit than the UK, where you can explore a wealth of haunted locations and experience the thrill of the unknown.

This guide is designed for those who want to explore the UK's haunted sites and indulge in paranormal tourism. In this book, you'll find detailed information on some of the most haunted locations in the UK, from ancient castles and cemeteries to hotels and pubs. Whether you're a seasoned ghost hunter or a curious traveller looking for a new adventure, this guide will provide you with all the information you need to plan your next paranormal trip.

Haunted Britain The Paranormal Tourist's UK Handbook includes a wide range of locations, each with its own unique history and ghostly sightings. You'll find information on the Tower of London, one of the most famous haunted locations in the world, as well as lesser-known sites like the Skirrid Inn in Wales, which has been in operation for over 900 years and is said to be haunted by the ghosts of executed prisoners.

In this guide, you'll also find practical information on each location, including directions, opening times, and admission fees. You'll learn about the history of each location, the reported ghost sightings, and the paranormal investigations that have taken place there. The guide also includes tips on how to conduct your own ghost hunt and what equipment you'll need to capture evidence of the paranormal.

Haunted Britain The Paranormal Tourist's UK Handbook is a resource for anyone interested in exploring the UK's haunted sites. Whether you're looking for a spooky adventure or hoping to connect with the spirit world, this guide will provide you with everything you need to plan an unforgettable paranormal trip. So, get ready to embark on a journey into the unknown and discover the secrets of the UK's most haunted places.

The Tower of London, London

The Tower of London, one of the most famous landmarks in London, has a reputation for being one of the most haunted places in the UK. The history of the Tower of London dates back to the Norman Conquest in 1066, and over the centuries, it has been used as a royal palace, a prison, a place of execution, and even a zoo. The Tower of London is said to be haunted by numerous ghosts and spirits, with some of the most famous being:

Anne Boleyn - The second wife of King Henry VIII was executed by beheading at the Tower in 1536. Her ghost is said to haunt the Chapel of St. Peter ad Vincula, where she was buried.

The Princes in the Tower - In 1483, two young boys, Edward V and his brother Richard, were imprisoned in the Tower and never seen again. It is said that their ghosts still haunt the White Tower.

Lady Jane Grey - The teenage queen who ruled England for just nine days before being imprisoned in the Tower and executed for treason. Her ghost is said to appear in the chapel where she is buried.

Thomas Becket - The Archbishop of Canterbury was murdered in 1170, and his ghost is said to haunt the Tower Green.

The Headless Drummer - This ghost is said to haunt the Martin Tower and is believed to be the ghost of a drummer boy who was killed by a sentry.

In addition to these famous ghosts, there have been reports of other ghostly sightings and supernatural occurrences at the Tower, including phantom footsteps, unexplained noises, and mysterious apparitions. Many believe that the history of the Tower, with its dark past of executions and imprisonment, has left an imprint on the place, making it a magnet for paranormal activity.

It's worth noting that there is no scientific evidence to support the existence of ghosts or supernatural phenomena, and many of the stories and legends surrounding the Tower of London may be based on folklore, hearsay, or exaggeration. However, the Tower's reputation as a haunted place has made it a popular destination for ghost hunters, paranormal investigators, and tourists seeking a thrill.

Hampton Court Palace, Surrey

Hampton Court Palace, located in Surrey, England, has a reputation for being one of the most haunted places in England. The palace was built in the early 16th century by Cardinal Thomas Wolsey, and later passed into the hands of King Henry VIII, who expanded and renovated it extensively. Over the centuries, numerous ghostly sightings and paranormal experiences have been reported at the palace.

One of the most famous ghosts at Hampton Court Palace is that of Catherine Howard, the fifth wife of King Henry VIII. Catherine was imprisoned at the palace before being executed for adultery, and her ghost is said to haunt the haunted gallery at the palace. Visitors have reported hearing her screams and footsteps, and some have even claimed to have seen her ghostly figure.

Another famous ghost at the palace is that of Sybil Penn, the nursemaid of Prince Edward, the son of King Henry VIII and his third wife, Jane Seymour. Sybil Penn's ghost is said to haunt the palace, and she has been seen carrying a baby in her arms.

In addition to these famous ghosts, there have been reports of other ghostly sightings and supernatural occurrences at the palace, including phantom footsteps, unexplained noises, and mysterious apparitions. Many believe that the history of the palace, with its dark past of executions and imprisonment, has left an imprint on the place, making it a magnet for paranormal activity.

The reasons for the haunting of Hampton Court Palace are not entirely clear. Some believe that the tragic events that took place within its walls have left an imprint on the building, while others believe that the palace's location on a ley line, a line of energy that some people believe to be linked to paranormal activity, may be a factor. In any case, the palace's reputation as a haunted place has made it a popular destination for ghost hunters, paranormal investigators, and tourists seeking a spooky thrill.

Edinburgh Castle, Scotland

Edinburgh Castle is one of the most famous and iconic landmarks in Scotland, located on a rocky hilltop in the heart of Edinburgh. The castle has a rich and complex history dating back to the 12th century and has served many purposes, including as a royal residence, a military barracks, and a prison. Over the centuries, numerous ghostly sightings and paranormal experiences have been reported at the castle, making it one of the most haunted places in Scotland.

One of the most famous ghosts at Edinburgh Castle is that of the piper who disappeared. According to legend, a piper was once sent to explore a tunnel beneath the castle and was instructed to play his bagpipes as he went so that his progress could be tracked. However, after a while, the music suddenly stopped, and the piper was never seen or heard from again. It is said that his ghost still haunts the castle, playing his bagpipes and leading visitors down the same tunnel he disappeared into.

Another famous ghost at the castle is that of a headless drummer boy. His ghost is said to appear at the castle every year on the anniversary of his death, drumming a ghostly beat before disappearing into thin air.

Other paranormal occurrences at Edinburgh Castle include ghostly apparitions, unexplained sounds and footsteps, and the feeling of being watched or touched by an unseen presence. Some visitors have reported seeing the ghost of a woman in a flowing gown, while others have claimed to have seen the ghost of a dog wandering the castle grounds.

The reasons for the haunting of Edinburgh Castle are not entirely clear, but many believe that the castle's turbulent history of war, violence, and death has left an imprint on the place, making it a magnet for paranormal activity. With its dark dungeons, secret tunnels, and storied past, Edinburgh Castle is a fascinating and eerie destination for those interested in the supernatural. Whether you're a sceptic or a believer, a visit to Edinburgh Castle is sure to send shivers down your spine.

The Ancient Ram Inn, Gloucestershire

The Ancient Ram Inn is a 12th-century building located in the village of Wotton-under-Edge in Gloucestershire, England. The inn has a reputation for being one of the most haunted places in the UK, with numerous ghostly sightings and paranormal occurrences reported over the years.

The inn's history is shrouded in mystery, but it is believed to have been built on the site of a former pagan burial ground. It has also been used as a former priest's house and was allegedly a site for satanic rituals during the 16th century.

One of the most famous ghosts at the Ancient Ram Inn is that of a young woman who was allegedly murdered by a satanic coven in one of the rooms. Her ghost has been seen and heard by numerous visitors, with reports of strange noises, cold spots, and the sound of footsteps on the stairs.

Other reported ghostly sightings at the inn include the ghost of a monk, a witch who was allegedly burned at the stake, and the ghost of a shepherd who hanged himself in the barn.
The inn's owner, John Humphries, has also reported experiencing a variety of paranormal occurrences over the years, including objects moving by themselves, ghostly figures appearing in photographs, and the feeling of being touched by unseen hands.

The reasons for the haunting of the Ancient Ram Inn are not entirely clear, but many believe that the inn's dark and violent history has left an imprint on the place, making it a magnet for paranormal activity. With its creepy atmosphere, eerie history, and numerous ghostly sightings, the Ancient Ram Inn is a popular destination for ghost hunters and paranormal enthusiasts. However, it's not for the faint of heart, as the inn is said to be one of the most haunted and terrifying places in the UK.

Highgate Cemetery, London

Highgate Cemetery is a famous Victorian cemetery located in the north of London, England. The cemetery opened in 1839 and quickly became a popular burial ground for some of the most prominent and wealthy families of the time. Over the years, numerous ghostly sightings and paranormal occurrences have been reported at the cemetery, making it one of the most haunted places in London.

One of the most famous ghosts at Highgate Cemetery is that of the "Highgate Vampire." In the 1970s, there were reports of a tall, dark figure with red eyes and a cape roaming the cemetery at night. Some people claimed that the figure was a vampire, while others suggested it was a ghost or a hoax. Despite numerous investigations, the true identity of the Highgate Vampire remains a mystery.

Other ghostly sightings at the cemetery include the ghost of a woman in white who has been seen wandering the cemetery grounds and the ghost of a man in a top hat who has been seen walking among the graves. Visitors have also reported feeling cold spots, hearing unexplained noises, and sensing the presence of unseen figures.

The reasons for the haunting of Highgate Cemetery are not entirely clear, but many believe that the cemetery's history and the numerous burials over the years have left an imprint on the place, making it a magnet for paranormal activity. With its eerie atmosphere, Victorian architecture, and numerous ghostly sightings, Highgate Cemetery is a popular destination for ghost hunters and paranormal enthusiasts.

However, it's important to note that the cemetery is a protected site and is not open to the public without prior permission. Visitors must book a tour to explore the cemetery and must follow strict rules to ensure the preservation of the site. Whether you believe in ghosts or not, Highgate Cemetery is a fascinating and eerie place that is steeped in history and legend.

Glamis Castle, Scotland

Glamis Castle is a historic castle located in Angus, Scotland. The castle has a long and fascinating history dating back to the 14th century, and it has been the subject of numerous ghost stories and legends over the years. It is said to be one of the most haunted places in Scotland.

One of the most famous ghosts at Glamis Castle is that of the "Grey Lady." Legend has it that the Grey Lady was a servant who fell in love with a nobleman and became pregnant with his child. When the nobleman rejected her, she hung herself from a tree in the castle grounds. Her ghost has been seen throughout the castle, particularly in the chapel and clock tower.

Another famous ghost at the castle is that of a young boy who was allegedly born with physical deformities and was locked away in a hidden room in the castle. His ghost is said to haunt the castle to this day, and visitors have reported feeling a sense of sadness and despair in his presence.

Other reported ghostly sightings at Glamis Castle include the ghost of a woman in a green dress, a phantom piper who plays his bagpipes in the castle's chapel, and the ghost of King Malcolm II, who is said to have been murdered at the castle in the 11th century.

The reasons for the haunting of Glamis Castle are not entirely clear, but many believe that the castle's long and turbulent history has left an imprint on the place, making it a magnet for paranormal activity. With its dark dungeons, hidden rooms, and countless tales of tragedy and intrigue, Glamis Castle is a fascinating and eerie destination for those interested in the supernatural.

Today, Glamis Castle is open to the public for tours, and visitors can explore the castle's history and legends for themselves. Whether you're a sceptic or a believer, a visit to Glamis Castle is sure to leave you with a sense of wonder and mystery.

Pendle Hill, Lancashire

Pendle Hill is a famous landmark located in Lancashire, England. It has a long history of witchcraft and paranormal activity and is believed to be one of the most haunted places in the UK.

The hill gained notoriety in the early 17th century when a group of twelve people were accused of witchcraft and tried in Lancaster. Ten of them were found guilty and executed, with many of the trials taking place on Pendle Hill. It is said that the spirits of these accused witches still haunt the area to this day.

In addition to the spirits of the executed witches, there have been numerous ghostly sightings and paranormal experiences reported at Pendle Hill. Visitors have reported feeling a sense of unease and dread, hearing unexplained noises and footsteps, and seeing ghostly apparitions.

One of the most famous ghost stories at Pendle Hill is that of the "White Lady." According to legend, the White Lady was a young woman who fell in love with a man who did not reciprocate her feelings. Heartbroken, she committed suicide by throwing herself off the top of Pendle Hill. Her ghost is said to haunt the area, and visitors have reported seeing her ghostly figure walking the hills.

The reasons for the haunting of Pendle Hill are not entirely clear, but many believe that the area's history of witchcraft and the tragic events that took place there have left an imprint on the place, making it a magnet for paranormal activity. With its eerie atmosphere, mysterious past, and numerous ghostly sightings, Pendle Hill is a popular destination for ghost hunters and paranormal enthusiasts.

Today, Pendle Hill is open to the public, and visitors can explore the area's history and legends for themselves. A visit to Pendle Hill is sure to leave you with a sense of wonder and mystery.

The London Dungeon, London

The London Dungeon is a popular tourist attraction located in London, England, that provides a dark and eerie recreation of London's dark and gruesome past. While the London Dungeon is a man-made attraction designed to scare and entertain visitors, it has also been the subject of numerous ghostly sightings and paranormal experiences.

One of the most famous ghosts at the London Dungeon is that of Anne Boleyn, the second wife of King Henry VIII, who was beheaded for treason in 1536. Anne Boleyn's ghost is said to haunt the London Dungeon, and visitors have reported seeing her ghostly figure in the corridors and chambers.

Other reported ghostly sightings at the London Dungeon include the ghost of a young girl who died of the plague, the ghost of a woman who was burned at the stake for witchcraft, and the ghost of a man who was hanged for his crimes.

The reasons for the haunting of the London Dungeon are not entirely clear, but many believe that the attraction's dark and gruesome subject matter has left an imprint on the place, making it a magnet for paranormal activity. With its eerie atmosphere, creepy exhibits, and numerous ghostly sightings, the London Dungeon is a popular destination for ghost hunters and paranormal enthusiasts.

It's important to note, however, that the London Dungeon is a man-made attraction, and while it may be scary and entertaining, it is not a true historical site. The ghostly sightings at the London Dungeon should be taken with a grain of salt and may be the result of the attraction's clever marketing and special effects. Nonetheless, the London Dungeon remains a popular destination for those looking for a spooky and thrilling experience in the heart of London.

The Skirrid Mountain Inn, Wales

The Skirrid Mountain Inn is a historic pub located in Abergavenny, Wales, that dates back to the 12th century. The inn has a reputation for being one of the most haunted places in Wales, with numerous ghostly sightings and paranormal occurrences reported over the years.

One of the most famous ghosts at the Skirrid Mountain Inn is that of the hanged man. According to legend, the inn was once used as a courthouse, and many people were sentenced to death by hanging on the premises. It is said that the ghosts of these executed men still haunt the inn, with many visitors reporting feeling the presence of a ghostly figure or hearing unexplained noises.

Other reported ghostly sightings at the Skirrid Mountain Inn include the ghost of a woman in Victorian dress who has been seen walking through the bar area, the ghost of a little girl who has been seen playing in one of the upstairs rooms, and the ghost of a monk who has been seen walking through the building.

The reasons for the haunting of the Skirrid Mountain Inn are not entirely clear, but many believe that the building's long and turbulent history has left an imprint on the place, making it a magnet for paranormal activity. With its dark and eerie atmosphere, rich history, and numerous ghostly sightings, the Skirrid Mountain Inn is a popular destination for ghost hunters and paranormal enthusiasts.

Today, the Skirrid Mountain Inn remains open to the public and serves as a popular pub and restaurant. Whether you're looking for a spooky experience or simply want to enjoy a pint in a historic setting, the Skirrid Mountain Inn is a fascinating and eerie destination that is sure to leave an impression.

Chillingham Castle, Northumberland

Chillingham Castle is a mediaeval castle located in Northumberland, England, that has a reputation for being one of the most haunted places in the UK. The castle dates back to the 12th century and has a long and fascinating history of battles, sieges, and royal visits.

One of the most famous ghosts at Chillingham Castle is that of the "blue boy." According to legend, a young boy was murdered in the castle in the 17th century and his ghost still haunts the Pink Room, where his body was discovered. Visitors have reported seeing a blue light and hearing a child's cry in the room, as well as feeling a chill in the air.

Another famous ghost at the castle is that of the White Lady. It is said that she was a woman who was imprisoned in the castle during the 14th century and was tortured and killed by her captors. Her ghost has been seen throughout the castle, and visitors have reported feeling a sense of unease in her presence.

Other reported ghostly sightings at Chillingham Castle include the ghost of a Spanish soldier who was killed during a siege, the ghost of a torturer who is said to haunt the dungeon, and the ghost of a young girl who died in the castle's chapel.

The reasons for the haunting of Chillingham Castle are not entirely clear, but many believe that the castle's violent history and tragic events have left an imprint on the place, making it a magnet for paranormal activity. With its dark and eerie atmosphere, mediaeval architecture, and numerous ghostly sightings, Chillingham Castle is a popular destination for ghost hunters and paranormal enthusiasts.

Today, Chillingham Castle is open to the public for tours, and visitors can explore the castle's history and legends for themselves. Whatever your beliefs, a visit to Chillingham Castle is sure to leave you with a sense of wonder and mystery.

Woodchester Mansion, Gloucestershire

Woodchester Mansion is a Gothic Revival mansion located in Woodchester Park in Gloucestershire, England. The mansion was built in the mid-19th century but was never completed, and today it stands as a striking but eerie reminder of a bygone era. It is also said to be one of the most haunted places in the UK.

One of the most famous ghosts at Woodchester Mansion is that of the "ghostly monk." Visitors have reported seeing a ghostly figure of a monk walking through the halls and corridors of the mansion, and some have even captured his image on camera.

Another ghostly sighting at Woodchester Mansion is that of a young girl. According to legend, she fell to her death from one of the upper floors of the mansion and her ghost still haunts the area to this day. Visitors have reported hearing her giggling and singing, as well as feeling a presence in the room where she died.

Other reported ghostly sightings at Woodchester Mansion include the ghost of a maid who is said to have been murdered by the mansion's owner, the ghost of a young woman who died of a broken heart, and the ghost of a Victorian gentleman who has been seen smoking a cigar in one of the rooms.

The reasons for the haunting of Woodchester Mansion are not entirely clear, but many believe that the building's turbulent history and the numerous tragedies that took place there have left an imprint on the place, making it a magnet for paranormal activity. With its eerie atmosphere, stunning architecture, and numerous ghostly sightings, Woodchester Mansion is a popular destination for ghost hunters and paranormal enthusiasts.

Today, Woodchester Mansion is open to the public for tours, and visitors can explore the mansion's history and legends for themselves. A visit to Woodchester Mansion is sure to leave you feeling a little on-edge.

Pluckley, Kent

Pluckley is a village located in the county of Kent in southeastern England. It is known for its many ghostly sightings and has been dubbed as the most haunted village in England.

One of the most famous ghostly sightings in Pluckley is that of the "red lady," who is said to haunt the local churchyard. Legend has it that the red lady was a woman who died during a fire at the nearby Dering Estate and was buried in the churchyard. Her ghostly figure has been seen walking through the churchyard at night, and some visitors have even reported feeling her cold breath on their necks.

Another famous ghost at Pluckley is that of the "watercress woman." It is said that she was a woman who died of hypothermia after selling watercress at the nearby Pinnock stream. Her ghost has been seen walking along the stream, and some visitors have reported hearing her voice calling out to them.

Other reported ghostly sightings in Pluckley include the ghost of a highwayman who was hanged near the village, the ghost of a schoolmaster who is said to have hanged himself in the schoolhouse, and the ghost of a soldier who was killed in battle during the English Civil War.

The reasons for the haunting of Pluckley are not entirely clear, but many believe that the village's long and tumultuous history has left an imprint on the place, making it a magnet for paranormal activity. With its quaint, picturesque setting, and numerous ghostly sightings, Pluckley is a popular destination for ghost hunters and paranormal enthusiasts.

Today, Pluckley remains a charming village that is open to visitors, and many people come to explore its history and legends.

Borley Rectory, Essex

Borley Rectory was a Victorian mansion located in the village of Borley in Essex, England. It was built in 1862 and became famous for its many ghostly sightings and paranormal activity.

One of the most famous ghosts at Borley Rectory was that of a nun who was said to have been involved in a love affair with a monk. It is said that they were both executed for their love, and their ghosts haunted the rectory for many years. Visitors have reported seeing the ghostly figure of the nun walking through the gardens and corridors of the mansion, as well as hearing unexplained noises and footsteps.

Another ghostly sighting at Borley Rectory was that of a coach and horses. According to legend, the coach was seen travelling along the driveway of the mansion, but when it reached the end, it vanished into thin air. Visitors have reported hearing the sound of hooves and carriage wheels at night, but when they investigate, there is nothing there.

Other reported ghostly sightings at Borley Rectory include the ghost of a headless man, the ghost of a nun who was bricked up alive, and the ghost of a young girl who died in a fire. There have also been reports of poltergeist activity, with objects moving and being thrown without explanation.

The reasons for the haunting of Borley Rectory are not entirely clear, but many believe that the mansion's long and troubled history has left an imprint on the place, making it a magnet for paranormal activity. With its eerie atmosphere, tragic history, and numerous ghostly sightings, Borley Rectory is a popular destination for ghost hunters and paranormal enthusiasts.

Today, Borley Rectory no longer stands, having been demolished in the 1940s. However, the legend and legacy of the mansion continue to fascinate and intrigue people, and many still visit the site to explore its history and legends.

Dartford Cemetery, Kent

Dartford Cemetery is a Victorian cemetery located in the town of Dartford in Kent, England. It is known for its many ghostly sightings and has a reputation as one of the most haunted cemeteries in the UK.

One of the most famous ghosts at Dartford Cemetery is that of a lady in white. According to legend, she was a woman who died in the 19th century and was buried in the cemetery. Her ghost has been seen walking through the cemetery at night, and some visitors have even reported feeling a cold breeze or seeing her face in the darkness.

Another famous ghostly sighting at Dartford Cemetery is that of a ghostly procession. Visitors have reported seeing a group of ghostly figures walking through the cemetery, dressed in Victorian clothing and carrying candles. It is said that this procession is made up of the ghosts of those buried in unmarked graves.

Other reported ghostly sightings at Dartford Cemetery include the ghost of a young boy who died in a car accident and has been seen playing in the cemetery, the ghost of a dog who has been seen running through the cemetery, and the ghost of a man who was buried in the cemetery after committing suicide.

The reasons for the haunting of Dartford Cemetery are not entirely clear, but many believe that the cemetery's long and tragic history has left an imprint on the place, making it a magnet for paranormal activity. With its eerie atmosphere, historic gravestones, and numerous ghostly sightings, Dartford Cemetery is a popular destination for ghost hunters and paranormal enthusiasts.

Today, Dartford Cemetery remains open to the public, and visitors can explore the cemetery's history and legends for themselves. A visit to Dartford Cemetery is sure to leave you with a sense of intrigue and fascination.

The Black Swan Hotel, North Yorkshire

The Black Swan Hotel is a historic coaching inn located in the market town of Helmsley in North Yorkshire, England. The hotel is known for its long and fascinating history, as well as its many ghostly sightings and paranormal activity.

One of the most famous ghosts at The Black Swan Hotel is that of a lady in white. It is said that she was a housekeeper at the hotel who died in the 19th century and has been seen walking through the halls and rooms of the hotel ever since. Visitors have reported feeling her presence, hearing unexplained noises, and even seeing her ghostly figure.

Another famous ghostly sighting at The Black Swan Hotel is that of a man in a top hat. It is said that he was a former guest at the hotel who died in the 19th century and has been seen walking through the hotel's courtyard. Visitors have also reported seeing his ghostly figure in the hotel's bar.

Other reported ghostly sightings at The Black Swan Hotel include the ghost of a young girl who has been seen playing in the hotel's corridors and the ghost of a former hotel owner who has been seen walking through the hotel's dining room.

The reasons for the haunting of The Black Swan Hotel are not entirely clear, but many believe that the hotel's long and fascinating history has left an imprint on the place, making it a magnet for paranormal activity. With its historic architecture, quaint setting, and numerous ghostly sightings, The Black Swan Hotel is a popular destination for ghost hunters and paranormal enthusiasts.

Today, The Black Swan Hotel remains open to the public, and visitors can explore the hotel's history and legends for themselves.

Berry Pomeroy Castle, Devon

Berry Pomeroy Castle is a ruined castle located in the village of Berry Pomeroy in Devon, England. It is known for its long and fascinating history, as well as its many ghostly sightings and paranormal activity.

One of the most famous ghosts at Berry Pomeroy Castle is that of the White Lady. According to legend, she was the daughter of one of the castle's former owners and fell in love with a knight who was not approved by her father. It is said that the knight was killed, and the White Lady was so grief-stricken that she died soon after. Her ghost has been seen wandering through the castle's ruins, and some visitors have even reported hearing her weeping.

Another famous ghostly sighting at Berry Pomeroy Castle is that of a young girl. It is said that she was the daughter of one of the castle's former owners and was kept hidden away in the castle's dungeons. Her ghost has been seen walking through the castle's ruins, and some visitors have even reported feeling her cold touch.

Other reported ghostly sightings at Berry Pomeroy Castle include the ghost of a cavalier who has been seen walking through the castle's gatehouse and the ghost of a man who was killed during a siege of the castle.

The reasons for the haunting of Berry Pomeroy Castle are not entirely clear, but many believe that the castle's long and tumultuous history, including numerous battles and sieges, has contributed to the paranormal activity reported there. With its atmospheric ruins, stunning views, and numerous ghostly sightings, Berry Pomeroy Castle is a popular destination for ghost hunters and paranormal enthusiasts.

Today, Berry Pomeroy Castle remains open to the public, and visitors can explore the castle's history and legends for themselves.

Castle Fraser, Aberdeenshire

Castle Fraser is a historic castle located in Aberdeenshire, Scotland. The castle dates back to the 15th century and is known for its long and fascinating history, as well as its many ghostly sightings and paranormal activity.

One of the most famous ghosts at Castle Fraser is that of a lady in green. According to legend, she was a former resident of the castle who died tragically. Her ghost has been seen walking through the castle's halls and rooms, and some visitors have even reported feeling her presence.

Another famous ghostly sighting at Castle Fraser is that of a ghostly couple. It is said that they were a couple who were caught in a storm and sought shelter in the castle. They were welcomed in and given a room for the night, but in the morning, they had vanished. Their ghostly figures have been seen walking through the castle's courtyard and gardens.

Other reported ghostly sightings at Castle Fraser include the ghost of a young girl who has been seen playing in the castle's corridors and the ghost of a former butler who has been seen walking through the castle's kitchen.

The reasons for the haunting of Castle Fraser are not entirely clear, but many believe that the castle's long and fascinating history, including its connections to the Jacobite uprising and the Fraser clan, has contributed to the paranormal activity reported there. With its historic architecture, beautiful gardens, and numerous ghostly sightings, Castle Fraser is a popular destination for ghost hunters and paranormal enthusiasts.

Tintagel Castle, Cornwall

Tintagel Castle is a mediaeval castle located on the rugged coastline of Cornwall, England. The castle is known for its long and fascinating history, as well as its many ghostly sightings and paranormal activity.

One of the most famous ghosts at Tintagel Castle is that of a beautiful woman known as the "White Lady." According to legend, she was a princess who lived in the castle and died tragically. Her ghost has been seen walking along the cliffs and ramparts of the castle, as well as in the castle's Great Hall.

Another famous ghostly sighting at Tintagel Castle is that of a headless man. It is said that he was a knight who died during a battle at the castle and has been seen wandering through the castle's ruins.

Other reported ghostly sightings at Tintagel Castle include the ghost of a monk who has been seen walking through the castle's chapel and the ghost of a small girl who has been seen playing in the castle's courtyard.

The reasons for the haunting of Tintagel Castle are not entirely clear, but many believe that the castle's long and tumultuous history, including its connections to the legendary King Arthur and the Dark Ages, has contributed to the paranormal activity reported there. With its stunning views, rugged coastline, and numerous ghostly sightings, Tintagel Castle is a popular destination for ghost hunters and paranormal enthusiasts.

Belgrave Hall, Leicestershire

Belgrave Hall is a historic house located in Leicestershire, England. The hall dates back to the 18th century and is known for its long and fascinating history, as well as its many ghostly sightings and paranormal activity.

One of the most famous ghosts at Belgrave Hall is that of a former owner, John Ellis. According to legend, he died in the house in the 18th century and has been seen walking through the hall's rooms and corridors. His ghost has been reported by visitors to the hall and by those who have lived in the building over the years.

Another famous ghostly sighting at Belgrave Hall is that of a ghostly figure known as the "Grey Lady." It is said that she was a former resident of the hall who died tragically. Her ghost has been seen walking through the hall's gardens and has been reported by visitors and staff alike.

Other reported ghostly sightings at Belgrave Hall include the ghost of a small girl who has been seen playing in the hall's corridors and the ghost of a man who was executed on the hall's grounds during the English Civil War.

Culloden Moor, Scotland

Culloden Moor is a historic battlefield located in Scotland. The site is known for the infamous Battle of Culloden that took place on 16 April 1746 between the Jacobites, led by Bonnie Prince Charlie, and the British Government forces, led by the Duke of Cumberland. The battle marked the end of the Jacobite rising of 1745 and the beginning of the Highland Clearances.

Culloden Moor is also known for its many ghostly sightings and paranormal activity. Visitors to the battlefield have reported seeing ghostly apparitions of soldiers, both Jacobite and British, dressed in period clothing and carrying weapons. The sounds of battle, including the clashing of swords and the firing of muskets, have also been reported by visitors to the site.

One of the most famous ghostly sightings at Culloden Moor is that of a woman in a blue dress. According to legend, she was a widow who came to the battlefield to search for her husband's body after the battle. Her ghost has been seen wandering through the battlefield, crying out for her lost love.

Another famous ghostly sighting at Culloden Moor is that of a drummer boy. It is said that he was a young boy who served in the Jacobite army and was killed during the battle. His ghost has been seen walking along the battlefield, playing his drum.

The reasons for the haunting of Culloden Moor are not entirely clear, but many believe that the trauma and violence of the battle have left an imprint on the site, making it a magnet for paranormal activity. With its atmospheric battlefield, historic monuments, and numerous ghostly sightings, Culloden Moor is a popular destination.

Craig-y-Nos Castle, Powys

Craig-y-Nos Castle is a historic castle located in the county of Powys in Wales. The castle dates back to the 19th century and is known for its long and fascinating history, as well as its many ghostly sightings and paranormal activity.

One of the most famous ghosts at Craig-y-Nos Castle is that of the former owner, Adelina Patti. Adelina was a world-famous opera singer who lived at the castle in the late 19th and early 20th centuries. She was known for her lavish parties and social events, and her ghost is said to still roam the halls of the castle, singing and entertaining guests.

Another famous ghostly sighting at Craig-y-Nos Castle is that of a ghostly figure known as the "Grey Lady." It is said that she was a former nurse who worked at the castle during World War II. Her ghost has been seen walking through the castle's corridors and rooms, and some visitors have even reported feeling her cold touch.

Other reported ghostly sightings at Craig-y-Nos Castle include the ghost of a young girl who has been seen playing in the castle's gardens and the ghost of a former stable boy who has been seen walking through the castle's stable block.

The reasons for the haunting of Craig-y-Nos Castle are not entirely clear, but many believe that the castle's long and fascinating history, including its connections to Adelina Patti and the World War II era, has contributed to the paranormal activity reported there. With its historic architecture, stunning views, and numerous ghostly sightings, Craig-y-Nos Castle is a popular destination for ghost hunters and paranormal enthusiasts.

The Jamaica Inn, Cornwall

The Jamaica Inn is a historic pub located on the rugged Bodmin Moor in Cornwall, England. The inn dates back to the 18th century and is known for its long and fascinating history, as well as its many ghostly sightings and paranormal activity.

One of the most famous ghosts at The Jamaica Inn is that of a smuggler who was killed on the inn's grounds. According to legend, he was betrayed by one of his fellow smugglers and was murdered in the inn's stable. His ghost has been seen walking through the inn's corridors and rooms, and some visitors have even reported feeling his presence.

Another famous ghostly sighting at The Jamaica Inn is that of a ghostly coach and horses. It is said that they were once used by smugglers to transport contraband goods along the moors. Their ghostly apparitions have been reported by visitors to the inn and have been seen galloping through the surrounding countryside.

Other reported ghostly sightings at The Jamaica Inn include the ghost of a young girl who has been seen playing in the inn's courtyard and the ghost of a former landlord who has been seen walking through the inn's bar.

The reasons for the haunting of The Jamaica Inn are not entirely clear, but many believe that the inn's long and fascinating history, including its connections to the smuggling trade and the local community, has contributed to the paranormal activity reported there. With its atmospheric pub, beautiful surroundings, and numerous ghostly sightings, The Jamaica Inn is a popular destination for ghost hunters and paranormal enthusiasts.

The Mermaid Inn, East Sussex

The Mermaid Inn is a historic pub and hotel located in the town of Rye in East Sussex, England. The inn dates back to the 15th century and is known for its long and fascinating history, as well as its many ghostly sightings and paranormal activity.

One of the most famous ghosts at The Mermaid Inn is that of a former smuggler known as "Hawkins." According to legend, he was a notorious smuggler who used the inn as a base for his illegal activities. His ghost has been seen walking through the inn's corridors and rooms, and some visitors have even reported feeling his presence.

Another famous ghostly sighting at The Mermaid Inn is that of a lady in white. It is said that she was a former resident of the inn who died tragically. Her ghost has been seen walking through the inn's corridors and rooms, and some visitors have reported feeling her icy touch.

Other reported ghostly sightings at The Mermaid Inn include the ghost of a former sailor who has been seen walking through the inn's bar and the ghost of a former housekeeper who has been seen in the inn's kitchen.

The reasons for the haunting of The Mermaid Inn are not entirely clear, but many believe that the inn's long and fascinating history, including its connections to the smuggling trade and the local community, has contributed to the paranormal activity reported there.

The Spaniards Inn, London

The Spaniards Inn is a historic pub located in Hampstead, London. The inn dates back to the 16th century and is known for its long and fascinating history, as well as its many ghostly sightings and paranormal activity.

One of the most famous ghosts at The Spaniards Inn is that of a former landlord, known as "Black Dick." According to legend, he was a notorious highwayman who used the inn as a base for his illegal activities. His ghost has been seen walking through the inn's corridors and rooms, and some visitors have even reported feeling his presence.

Another famous ghostly sighting at The Spaniards Inn is that of a woman in white. It is said that she was a former resident of the inn who died tragically. Her ghost has been seen walking through the inn's garden and has been reported by visitors and staff alike.

Other reported ghostly sightings at The Spaniards Inn include the ghost of a former stable boy who has been seen in the inn's courtyard and the ghost of a former patron who has been seen in the inn's bar.

The reasons for the haunting of The Spaniards Inn are not entirely clear, but many believe that the inn's long and fascinating history, including its connections to the highwayman Black Dick, has contributed to the paranormal activity reported there. With its historic architecture, beautiful gardens, and numerous ghostly sightings, The Spaniards Inn is a popular destination for ghost hunters.

Mary King's Close, Edinburgh

Mary King's Close is a narrow street located in the Old Town of Edinburgh, Scotland. The close dates back to the 16th century and is known for its dark and fascinating history, as well as its many ghostly sightings and paranormal activity.

One of the most famous ghosts at Mary King's Close is that of a young girl named Annie. According to legend, Annie was a victim of the plague and died in one of the close's underground chambers. Her ghost has been seen walking through the close's narrow streets and has been reported by visitors and staff alike.

Another famous ghostly sighting at Mary King's Close is that of a former resident known as "Mr. Boots." It is said that he was a wealthy merchant who lived in the close during the 17th century. His ghost has been seen walking through the close's underground chambers and has been reported by visitors and staff alike.

Other reported ghostly sightings at Mary King's Close include the ghost of a young boy who has been seen playing in one of the close's underground chambers and the ghost of a former resident who has been seen walking through the close's narrow streets.

The Theatre Royal, Drury Lane, London

The Theatre Royal, Drury Lane is a historic theatre located in Covent Garden, London. The theatre dates back to the 17th century and is known for its long and fascinating history, as well as its many ghostly sightings and paranormal activity.

One of the most famous ghosts at The Theatre Royal, Drury Lane is that of a former actor named Joseph Grimaldi. He was a famous clown who performed at the theatre during the 19th century. His ghost has been seen walking through the theatre's corridors and dressing rooms, and some visitors have even reported hearing his laughter echoing through the building.

Another famous ghostly sighting at The Theatre Royal, Drury Lane is that of a former theatre manager, known as "The Man in Grey." It is said that he was a former patron of the theatre who died tragically. His ghost has been seen walking through the theatre's upper circle and has been reported by visitors and staff alike.

Other reported ghostly sightings at The Theatre Royal, Drury Lane include the ghost of a former actress who has been seen walking through the theatre's wings and the ghost of a former patron who has been seen sitting in the theatre's stalls.

The reasons for the haunting of The Theatre Royal, Drury Lane are not entirely clear, but many believe that the theatre's long and fascinating history, including its connections to famous actors and performances, has contributed to the paranormal activity reported there. With its beautiful architecture, stunning productions, and numerous ghostly sightings, The Theatre Royal, Drury Lane is a popular destination for theatre-goers and paranormal enthusiasts alike.

The Castle of Mey, Scotland

The Castle of Mey is a historic castle located in the northernmost tip of Scotland. The castle dates back to the 16th century and is known for its long and fascinating history, as well as its many ghostly sightings and paranormal activity.

One of the most famous ghosts at The Castle of Mey is that of a former butler, known as "The Grey Lady." It is said that she was a former resident of the castle who died tragically. Her ghost has been seen walking through the castle's corridors and has been reported by visitors and staff alike.

Another famous ghostly sighting at The Castle of Mey is that of a former gardener, known as "The Green Lady." It is said that she was a former employee of the castle who died tragically. Her ghost has been seen walking through the castle's gardens and has been reported by visitors and staff alike.

Other reported ghostly sightings at The Castle of Mey include the ghost of a former resident who has been seen walking through the castle's rooms and the ghost of a former servant who has been seen in the castle's kitchens.

The reasons for the haunting of The Castle of Mey are not entirely clear, but many believe that the castle's long and fascinating history, including its connections to the royal family, has contributed to the paranormal activity reported there.

With its beautiful architecture, stunning gardens, and numerous ghostly sightings, The Castle of Mey is a popular destination for history buffs and paranormal enthusiasts alike.

The Ragged School Museum, London

The Ragged School Museum is a historic site located in Mile End, London. The museum dates back to the 19th century and is known for its long and fascinating history, as well as its many ghostly sightings and paranormal activity.

The museum is housed in a former school building, which was originally established to provide education for poor and underprivileged children in the East End of London. The building has since been restored and transformed into a museum, which tells the story of the school and its students.

However, the history of the building is not the only thing that visitors to the Ragged School Museum can experience. Many visitors and staff members have reported strange and unexplained occurrences within the building, leading some to believe that the museum is haunted.

One of the most famous ghostly sightings at the Ragged School Museum is that of a young girl named Esther. According to legend, Esther was a former student of the school who died tragically. Her ghost has been seen walking through the museum's corridors and has been reported by visitors and staff alike.

Another famous ghostly sighting at the Ragged School Museum is that of a former teacher, known as "The Lady in Grey."

It is said that she was a former teacher at the school who died tragically. Her ghost has been seen walking through the museum's classrooms and has been reported by visitors and staff alike.

Other reported ghostly sightings at the Ragged School Museum include the ghost of a former student who has been seen playing in the museum's playground and the ghost of a former caretaker who has been seen in the museum's basement.

The reasons for the haunting of the Ragged School Museum are not entirely clear, but many believe that the building's long and fascinating history, including its connections to the education of underprivileged children, has contributed to the paranormal activity reported there. With its historic architecture, interactive exhibits, and numerous ghostly sightings, the Ragged School Museum is a popular destination for history buffs and paranormal enthusiasts alike.

Whether you're a sceptic or a believer, a visit to the Ragged School Museum is sure to leave you with a sense of intrigue and wonder. As you explore the museum's exhibits and learn about its fascinating history, keep your eyes and ears open for any signs of the paranormal activity that has been reported there. Who knows, you may just have your own ghostly encounter at the Ragged School Museum!

The Beechwood House, Leicestershire

Beechwood House is a historic mansion located in the heart of Leicestershire, England. The house dates back to the 18th century and is known for its long and fascinating history, as well as its many ghostly sightings and paranormal activity.

One of the most famous ghostly sightings at Beechwood House is that of a former housemaid, known as "The Lady in Grey." It is said that she was a former employee of the house who died tragically. Her ghost has been seen walking through the house's corridors and has been reported by visitors.

Another famous ghostly sighting at Beechwood House is that of a former owner, known as "The Lady in Black." It is said that she was a former resident of the house who died tragically. Her ghost has been seen walking through the house's rooms and has been reported by visitors and staff alike.

Other reported ghostly sightings at Beechwood House include the ghost of a former servant who has been seen walking through the house's kitchen and the ghost of a former resident who has been seen in the house's gardens.

The reasons for the haunting of Beechwood House are not entirely clear, but many believe that the house's long and fascinating history, including its connections to the local community, has contributed to the paranormal activity reported there.

Harrow School, London

Harrow School, located in the London Borough of Harrow, is one of the most prestigious schools in the UK. Founded in 1572, the school has a long and storied history, with many tales of ghosts and paranormal activity. In this blog post, we'll explore the haunted history of Harrow School.

One of the most famous ghost stories associated with Harrow School is that of a former teacher, known as "The Headless Master." According to legend, this teacher was beheaded during the English Civil War, and his ghost has been seen walking through the school's corridors, dressed in his old-fashioned clothes and carrying his head under his arm.

Another famous ghostly sighting at Harrow School is that of a former student, known as "The Grey Ghost." It is said that this student died tragically in the school's attic, and his ghost has been seen wandering the halls of the school, dressed in his old school uniform.

Other reported ghostly sightings at Harrow School include the ghost of a former headmaster who has been seen walking through the school's classrooms and the ghost of a former student who has been seen playing in the school's chapel.

The reasons for the haunting of Harrow School are not entirely clear, but many believe that the school's long and fascinating history, including its connections to famous alumni such as Winston Churchill, has contributed to the paranormal activity reported there. With its beautiful architecture, rich history, and numerous ghostly sightings, Harrow School is a popular destination for ghost hunters and paranormal enthusiasts.

Today, Harrow School remains open to the public, and visitors can explore the school's history and legends for themselves. Whether you're a sceptic or a believer, a visit to Harrow School is sure to leave you with a sense of intrigue and wonder. As you wander the halls and corridors of this historic institution, keep your eyes and ears open for any signs of the paranormal activity that has been reported there.

The Old Rectory, Essex

The Old Rectory is a historic building located in the county of Essex, England. Built in the 18th century, the house is known for its long and fascinating history, as well as its many ghostly sightings and paranormal activity.

One of the most famous ghostly sightings at The Old Rectory is that of a former resident, known as "The White Lady." It is said that she was a former owner of the house who died tragically. Her ghost has been seen walking through the house's corridors and has been reported by staff.

Another famous ghostly sighting at The Old Rectory is that of a former gardener, known as "The Green Man." It is said that he was a former employee of the house who died tragically. His ghost has been seen walking through the house's gardens and has been reported by visitors and staff alike.

Other reported ghostly sightings at The Old Rectory include the ghost of a former maid who has been seen walking through the house's bedrooms and the ghost of a former owner who has been seen in the house's library.

The reasons for the haunting of The Old Rectory are not entirely clear, but many believe that the house's long and fascinating history, including its connections to the local community, has contributed to the paranormal activity reported there. With its beautiful architecture, stunning gardens, and numerous ghostly sightings, The Old Rectory is a popular destination for history buffs and paranormal enthusiasts alike.

Royal Exchange Theatre, Manchester

The Royal Exchange Theatre in Manchester, England is one of the city's most iconic cultural landmarks, and is known for its long and fascinating history, as well as its many ghostly sightings and paranormal activity.

The theatre was originally built in 1874 as the Royal Exchange, a hub of commerce where traders and merchants would come together to conduct business. It was later transformed into a theatre in 1976 and has since become a beloved institution in the Manchester arts scene.

However, the history of the Royal Exchange Theatre is not the only thing that visitors can experience. Many visitors and staff members have reported strange and unexplained occurrences within the building, leading some to believe that the theatre is haunted.

One of the most famous ghostly sightings at the Royal Exchange Theatre is that of a former stagehand, known as "The Grey Lady." According to legend, she was a former employee of the theatre who died tragically in a fall from the theatre's catwalk. Her ghost has been seen walking through the theatre's corridors and has been reported by visitors and staff alike.

Another famous ghostly sighting at the Royal Exchange Theatre is that of a former performer, known as "The Lady in Black." It is said that she was a former actor who died tragically while performing on stage. Her ghost has been seen walking through the theatre's dressing rooms and has been reported by visitors and staff alike.

Other reported ghostly sightings at the Royal Exchange Theatre include the ghost of a former manager who has been seen walking through the theatre's offices and the ghost of a former audience member who has been seen in the theatre's seating areas.

The reasons for the haunting of the Royal Exchange Theatre are not entirely clear, but many believe that the building's long and fascinating history, including its connections to the local community and the performing arts, has contributed to the paranormal activity reported there.

St. Botolph's Church, Lincolnshire

St. Botolph's Church, located in the historic market town of Boston, Lincolnshire, is one of the most famous and fascinating haunted sites in England. The church, which dates back to the 14th century, has a rich and storied history, and many visitors and locals have reported unexplained and eerie occurrences within its walls.

One of the most famous ghostly sightings at St. Botolph's Church is that of a former rector, known as "The Black Monk." According to legend, he was a former rector who died tragically in the church after being excommunicated for his sins. His ghost has been seen wandering the church's corridors and has been reported by visitors and staff alike.

Another famous ghostly sighting at St. Botolph's Church is that of a former choirboy, known as "The Brown Boy." It is said that he was a former choirboy who died tragically in the church after being struck by lightning. His ghost has been seen in the church's bell tower and has been reported by visitors and staff alike.

Other reported ghostly sightings at St. Botolph's Church includes the ghost of a former nun who has been seen in the church's chapel and the ghost of a former soldier who has been seen in the church's graveyard.

The reasons for the haunting of St. Botolph's Church are not entirely clear, but many believe that the church's long and fascinating history, including its connections to the local community and the religious practices of the time, has contributed to the paranormal activity reported there. With its stunning architecture, beautiful stained-glass windows, and numerous ghostly sightings, St. Botolph's Church is a popular destination for history buffs and paranormal enthusiasts.

Today, St. Botolph's Church remains open to the public, and visitors can explore the church's history and legends for themselves. Whether you're a believer or not, a visit to St. Botolph's Church is sure to leave you with a sense of intrigue and wonder.

As you wander the halls and corridors of this historic church, keep your eyes and ears open for any signs of the paranormal activity that has been reported there. Who knows, you may just have your own ghostly encounter at St. Botolph's Church!

Gwydir Castle, Conwy

Gwydir Castle, located in the county of Conwy, Wales, is a stunningly beautiful castle with a long and storied history. However, it is not just the castle's history that draws visitors - many believe that Gwydir Castle is haunted.

One of the most famous ghostly sightings at Gwydir Castle is that of a former owner, known as "The Grey Lady." According to legend, she was a former resident of the castle who died by falling down the stairs. Her ghost has been seen wandering the castle's corridors, and has been reported by visitors and staff alike.

Another famous ghostly sighting at Gwydir Castle is that of a former servant, known as "The Maid." It is said that she was a former servant who died tragically in the castle's kitchens. Her ghost has been seen in the castle's kitchens, and has been reported by visitors and staff alike.

Other reported ghostly sightings at Gwydir Castle include the ghost of a former owner who has been seen in the castle's drawing room, and the ghost of a former gardener who has been seen in the castle's gardens.

Michelham Priory, East Sussex

Michelham Priory, located in the picturesque county of East Sussex, England, is a beautiful and historic site with a long and fascinating history. However, it is not just the priory's history that draws visitors - many believe that Michelham Priory is haunted.

One of the most famous ghostly sightings at Michelham Priory is that of a former owner, known as "The Grey Lady." According to legend, she was a former resident of the priory who died tragically in a fire. Her ghost has been seen walking through the priory's corridors, and has been reported by visitors and staff alike.

Another famous ghostly sighting at Michelham Priory is that of a former monk, known as "The Monk." It is said that he was a former resident of the priory who died tragically in the Black Death. His ghost has been seen walking through the priory's gardens, and has been reported by visitors and staff alike.

Other reported ghostly sightings at Michelham Priory include the ghost of a former prioress who has been seen in the priory's chapel, and the ghost of a former gardener who has been seen in the priory's gardens.

The reasons for the haunting of Michelham Priory are not entirely clear. However, many believe that the priory's long and fascinating history.

That includes its connections to the local community and the religious practices of the time, has contributed to the paranormal activity reported there. With its stunning architecture, beautiful gardens, and numerous ghostly sightings, Michelham Priory is a popular destination for history buffs and paranormal enthusiasts alike.

Castle Rising, Norfolk

Castle Rising, located in the county of Norfolk, England, is a historic castle that dates back to the 12th century. It is one of the most iconic and recognizable castles in England, and has a fascinating and complex history. However, the castle's history is not the only thing that draws visitors - many believe that Castle Rising is haunted.

One of the most famous ghostly sightings at Castle Rising is that of a former owner, known as "The White Lady." According to legend, she was a former resident of the castle who died tragically in childbirth. Her ghost has been seen walking through the castle's corridors, and has been reported by visitors and staff alike.

Another famous ghostly sighting at Castle Rising is that of a former owner, known as "The Brown Lady." It is said that she was a former resident of the castle who died tragically in a fire. Her ghost has been seen walking through the castle's halls, and has been reported by visitors and staff alike.

Other reported ghostly sightings at Castle Rising include the ghost of a former servant who has been seen in the castle's kitchens, and the ghost of a former owner who has been seen in the castle's gardens.

The reasons for the haunting of Castle Rising are not entirely clear, but many believe that the castle's long and fascinating history, including its connections to the local community and the political and social changes of the time, has contributed to the paranormal activity reported there.

With its stunning architecture, beautiful gardens, and numerous ghostly sightings, Castle Rising is a popular destination for history buffs and paranormal enthusiasts alike.

Today, Castle Rising remains open to the public, and visitors can explore the castle's history and legends for themselves. Whether you're a believer or otherwise, a visit to Castle Rising is sure to leave you with a sense of intrigue and wonder. As you wander the halls and gardens of this historic castle, keep your eyes and ears open for any signs of the paranormal activity that has been reported there.

The Edinburgh Vaults, Edinburgh

The Edinburgh Vaults, located beneath the city of Edinburgh in Scotland, are a series of tunnels and chambers that were built in the late 18th century. These underground chambers were used for a variety of purposes, including storage and as living quarters for the city's poorest inhabitants. However, the vaults have a darker history - many believe that they are haunted.

One of the most famous ghostly sightings in the Edinburgh Vaults is that of a former woman, known as "Annie." According to legend, she was a former resident of the vaults who died tragically in childbirth. Her ghost has been seen walking through the vaults, and has been reported by visitors and staff alike.

Another famous ghostly sighting in the Edinburgh Vaults is that of a former merchant, known as "The Watcher." It is said that he was a former resident of the vaults who was murdered for his wealth. His ghost has been seen watching over the vaults, and has been reported by visitors and staff alike.

Other reported ghostly sightings in the Edinburgh Vaults include the ghost of a former worker who has been seen in the vaults' brickwork, and the ghost of a former child who has been seen playing in the vaults' chambers.

The reasons for the haunting of the Edinburgh Vaults are not entirely clear.

Still, many believe that the dark and squalid conditions that the inhabitants of the vaults were forced to endure, as well as the tragic deaths and violence that occurred there, have contributed to the paranormal activity. With its eerie atmosphere and numerous ghostly sightings, the Edinburgh Vaults are a popular destination for history buffs and paranormal enthusiasts alike.

Today, the Edinburgh Vaults remain open to the public, and visitors can explore the vaults' history and legends for themselves. Whether you're a sceptic or a believer, a visit to the Edinburgh Vaults is sure to leave you with a sense of intrigue and wonder.

The Beech Hill Hotel, Cumbria

The Beech Hill Hotel, located in the beautiful county of Cumbria in England, is a stunningly beautiful hotel that dates back to the 1900s. It sits on the shore of Lake Windermere, one of the most picturesque lakes in the world. However, it is not just the hotel's history and stunning location that draw visitors - many believe that The Beech Hill Hotel is haunted.

One of the most famous ghostly sightings at The Beech Hill Hotel is that of a former owner, known as "The Grey Lady." According to legend, she was a former resident of the hotel who died long ago. Her ghost has been seen walking through the hotel's corridors and has been reported by visitors and staff.

Another famous ghostly sighting at The Beech Hill Hotel is that of a former servant, known as "The Maid." It is said that she was a former servant who died tragically in the hotel's kitchen. Her ghost has been seen in the hotel's kitchen, and has been reported by visitors and staff alike.

Other reported ghostly sightings at The Beech Hill Hotel include the ghost of a former guest who has been seen in one of the hotel's rooms and the ghost of a former worker who has been seen in the hotel's gardens.

The reasons for the haunting of The Beech Hill Hotel are not entirely clear, but many believe that the hotel's long and fascinating history, including its connections to the local community.

Also, the natural beauty of the surrounding area, has contributed to the paranormal activity reported there. With its stunning architecture, beautiful gardens, and numerous ghostly sightings, The Beech Hill Hotel is a popular destination for history buffs and paranormal enthusiasts alike.

Today, The Beech Hill Hotel remains open to the public, and visitors can explore the hotel's history and legends for themselves. Whether you're a sceptic or a believer, a visit to The Beech Hill Hotel is sure to leave you with a sense of intrigue and wonder. As you wander the halls and gardens of this historic hotel, keep your eyes and ears open for any signs of the paranormal activity that has been reported there.

Glamorgan Building, Cardiff

The Glamorgan Building, located in the heart of Cardiff in Wales, is a historic building that dates back to the early 20th century. It is a stunning example of Victorian architecture, with its ornate façade and grand entrance hall. However, the building's history is not the only thing that draws visitors - many believe that the Glamorgan Building is haunted.

One of the most famous ghostly sightings at the Glamorgan Building is that of a former resident, known as "The Lady in Grey." According to legend, she was a former teacher at the building who died tragically in a fire. Her ghost has been seen walking through the building's corridors.

Another famous ghostly sighting at the Glamorgan Building is that of a former student, known as "The Shadow Man." It is said that he was a former student who committed suicide in the building. His ghost has been seen in the building's stairwells, and has been reported by visitors and staff alike.

Other reported ghostly sightings at the Glamorgan Building include the ghost of a former professor who has been seen in one of the building's lecture halls, and the ghost of a former janitor who has been seen in the building's basement.

The Royal Hippodrome Theatre, East Sussex

The Royal Hippodrome Theatre, located in East Sussex, England, is a historic building that has been entertaining audiences since the early 1900s. It is known for its stunning architecture and impressive performances. However, many believe that The Royal Hippodrome Theatre is haunted.

One of the most famous ghostly sightings at The Royal Hippodrome Theatre is that of a former performer, known as "The Lady in White." According to legend, she was a former singer at the theatre who died tragically during a performance. Her ghost has been seen walking through the theatre's corridors and has been reported by visitors and staff alike.

Another famous ghostly sighting at The Royal Hippodrome Theatre is that of a former stagehand, known as "The Poltergeist." It is said that he was a former employee at the theatre who died tragically while working on the stage. His ghost has been seen moving props and equipment on the stage, and has been reported by visitors and staff alike.

Other reported ghostly sightings at The Royal Hippodrome Theatre include the ghost of a former audience member who has been seen sitting in the theatre's seats, and the ghost of a former actor who has been seen on stage.

The reasons for the haunting of The Royal Hippodrome Theatre are not entirely clear, but many believe that the theatre's long and fascinating history, including its connections to the local community and the entertainment industry, has contributed to the paranormal activity reported there. With its stunning architecture, rich history, and numerous ghostly sightings, The Royal Hippodrome Theatre is a popular destination for history buffs and paranormal enthusiasts

Pengersick Castle, Cornwall

Pengersick Castle, located in Cornwall, England, is a historic building that dates back to the 16th century. It is known for its unique architecture and fascinating history. However, many believe that Pengersick Castle is haunted.

One of the most famous ghostly sightings at Pengersick Castle is that of a former resident, known as "The White Girl." According to legend, she was a former resident of the castle who died tragically. Her ghost has been seen walking through the castle's corridors and has been reported by visitors and staff alike.

Another famous ghostly sighting at Pengersick Castle is that of a former owner, known as "The Black Monk." It is said that he was a former owner of the castle who died tragically during a battle. His ghost has been seen in the castle's courtyard and has been reported by visitors and staff alike.

Other reported ghostly sightings at Pengersick Castle include the ghost of a former servant who has been seen in one of the castle's rooms and the ghost of a former prisoner who has been seen in the castle's dungeon.

The reasons for the haunting of Pengersick Castle are not entirely clear, but many believe that the castle's long and fascinating history, including its connections to the local community and the numerous battles that took place nearby, has contributed to the paranormal activity reported there. With its unique architecture, rich history, and numerous ghostly sightings, Pengersick Castle is a popular destination for history buffs and paranormal enthusiasts alike.

Today, Pengersick Castle remains open to the public, and visitors can explore the castle's history and legends for themselves.

The New Inn, Gloucestershire

The New Inn, located in the town of Gloucester in Gloucestershire, England, is a historic building that dates back to the 15th century. It has served as an inn for many centuries, and is known for its charming architecture and cosy atmosphere. However, many believe that The New Inn is haunted, and there have been numerous reported sightings of ghosts and other paranormal activity in the building.

One of the most famous ghostly sightings at The New Inn is that of a former resident, known as "The Lady in Blue." According to legend, she was a former resident of the inn who died tragically in a fire. Her ghost has been seen walking through the inn's corridors and has been reported by visitors and staff alike.

Another famous ghostly sighting at The New Inn is that of a former landlord, known as "The Grey Lady." It is said that she was a former landlord of the inn who died tragically during a renovation project. Her ghost has been seen in the inn's courtyard.

Other reported ghostly sightings at The New Inn include the ghost of a former servant who has been seen in one of the inn's rooms, and the ghost of a former soldier who has been seen in the inn's bar.

One particularly spooky story about The New Inn involves a group of guests who reported hearing footsteps and whispering in one of the inn's rooms. When they investigated, they found that the room was completely empty, but the whispers continued. Another guest reported seeing a figure walking through the inn's courtyard, even though no one else was present.

The reasons for the haunting of The New Inn are not entirely clear, but many believe that the building's long and fascinating history, including its connections to the local community and the many travellers who have passed through its doors, has contributed to the paranormal activity reported there. With its charming architecture, cosy atmosphere, and numerous ghostly sightings, The New Inn is a popular destination for history buffs and paranormal enthusiasts alike.

The Pergola, Hampstead Heath, London

The Pergola is a stunning garden feature located in Hampstead Heath, London, and is known for its beautiful architecture and tranquil atmosphere. However, many people believe that The Pergola is haunted, and there have been numerous reported sightings of ghosts and other paranormal activity in the area.

One of the most famous ghostly sightings at The Pergola is that of a woman dressed in white. She is said to appear at night and walk along the pergola's paths, disappearing into the mist. Some have claimed that she is the ghost of a former resident of the area who died tragically in a fire.

Another famous ghostly sighting at The Pergola is that of a man who is said to appear at the entrance to the pergola. He is described as being dressed in clothing from the early 1900s and has been seen staring out at the surrounding area before disappearing without a trace.

There have also been reports of eerie sensations and strange sounds in the area, including footsteps and whispers, even when no one else is around.

One allegedly true story involves a group of friends who were exploring The Pergola late at night. They reported feeling a cold presence around them and heard strange noises, including footsteps and whispers. Suddenly, one of the group members felt a cold hand touch their shoulder, but when they turned around, no one was there.

Another allegedly true story involves a couple who were walking through The Pergola when they saw a woman in white walking towards them. As she got closer, they realised that she was not solid and appeared to be a ghostly apparition. They quickly left the area, feeling unnerved by the experience.

The Warren, Bristol

The Warren, located in the city of Bristol in England, is a historic building that dates back to the 1800s. It has served as a hospital and asylum for many years, and is known for its eerie atmosphere and reputation for being haunted.

One of the most famous ghostly sightings at The Warren is that of a former patient, known as "The Lady in White." According to legend, she was a former patient of the asylum who died tragically while undergoing treatment. Her ghost has been seen walking through the asylum's corridors and has been reported by visitors and staff alike.

Another famous ghostly sighting at The Warren is that of a former doctor, known as "The Black Doctor." It is said that he was a former doctor at the asylum who was known for his cruel treatment of patients. His ghost has been seen in the asylum's courtyard and has been reported by visitors and staff alike.

Other reported ghostly sightings at The Warren include the ghost of a former nurse who has been seen in one of the asylum's rooms and the ghost of a former patient who has been seen wandering the halls.

One particularly spooky story about The Warren involves a group of paranormal investigators who were exploring the asylum late at night. They reported hearing strange noises and seeing unexplained shadows moving across the walls. Suddenly, one of the investigators felt a cold hand touch their shoulder, but when they turned around, no one was there.

The reasons for the haunting of The Warren are not entirely clear, but many believe that the building's long and fascinating history, including its connections to the local community and the numerous patients who were treated there over the years, has contributed to the paranormal activity reported there. With its eerie atmosphere and numerous ghostly sightings, The Warren is a popular destination for history buffs and paranormal enthusiasts alike.

Muncaster Castle, Cumbria

Muncaster Castle is a historic castle located in the Lake District in Cumbria, England. It is known for its stunning architecture and beautiful gardens, as well as its reputation for being one of the most haunted castles in the country. There have been numerous reported sightings of ghosts and other paranormal activity at the castle over the years.

One of the most famous ghostly sightings at Muncaster Castle is that of Tom Fool, a former court jester who is said to haunt the castle to this day. Visitors and staff have reported seeing his ghostly apparition in various parts of the castle, and some have claimed to have heard his eerie laughter echoing through the halls.

Another famous ghostly sighting at Muncaster Castle is that of a former housekeeper, known as "The White Lady." According to legend, she was a former housekeeper who died tragically after falling down a flight of stairs. Her ghost has been seen walking through the castle's corridors and has been reported by visitors and staff alike.

Other reported ghostly sightings at Muncaster Castle include the ghost of a former gardener who has been seen tending to the castle's gardens and the ghost of a former lady of the castle who has been seen walking through the castle's halls.

One particularly eerie story about Muncaster Castle involves a group of guests who were staying in one of the castle's bedrooms. They reported feeling a cold presence in the room and heard strange noises, including footsteps and whispers. Suddenly, the room grew extremely cold, and the group saw the ghostly apparition of a woman standing at the foot of their bed.

The Ancient Yew of Crowhurst, East Sussex

The Ancient Yew of Crowhurst is a famous tree located in the village of Crowhurst in East Sussex, England. The tree is believed to be over 1,000 years old and has long been associated with supernatural activity and paranormal sightings.

One of the most famous ghostly sightings associated with the Ancient Yew is that of a ghostly monk who has been seen walking through the nearby churchyard. Legend has it that the monk was once a member of the clergy who was buried near the tree and has returned as a ghost to guard the area.

Another famous ghostly sighting associated with the Ancient Yew is that of a ghostly lady who has been seen walking through the nearby fields. According to local legend, the lady was a former resident of the area who died tragically and has returned as a ghost to haunt the area.

Other reported paranormal activity associated with the Ancient Yew includes unexplained cold spots, eerie sensations, and strange noises.

Bodelwyddan Castle, Denbighshire

Bodelwyddan Castle is a historic castle located in Denbighshire, North Wales. The castle dates back to the 15th century and is known for its stunning architecture, beautiful gardens, and rich history. It is also well-known for its reputation as one of the most haunted castles in Wales.

One of the most famous ghostly sightings at Bodelwyddan Castle is that of a former soldier, known as "The Man in Grey." According to legend, he was a former soldier who died tragically during the Civil War and has been seen walking through the castle's corridors in his grey uniform.

Another famous ghostly sighting at Bodelwyddan Castle is that of a former maid, known as "The Grey Lady." Legend has it that she was a former maid at the castle who died tragically after falling in love with a member of the aristocracy. Her ghost has been seen walking through the castle's halls and has been reported by visitors and staff alike.

Other reported ghostly sightings at Bodelwyddan Castle include the ghost of a former housekeeper who has been seen tending to the castle's bedrooms and the ghost of a former stable hand who has been seen walking through the castle's courtyard.

One particularly spooky story about Bodelwyddan Castle involves a group of visitors who were exploring the castle late at night. They reported hearing strange noises and seeing unexplained shadows moving across the walls. Suddenly, one of the group members felt a cold hand touch their shoulder, but when they turned around, no one was there.

The reasons for the haunting of Bodelwyddan Castle are not entirely clear, but many believe that the building's long and fascinating history, including its connections to the local community and the numerous people who have lived and died there over the years, has contributed to the paranormal activity reported there. With its stunning architecture, beautiful gardens, and numerous ghostly sightings, Bodelwyddan Castle is a popular destination for history buffs and paranormal enthusiasts alike.

Erasmus Darwin House, Staffordshire

Erasmus Darwin House is a historic house located in Lichfield, Staffordshire, England. It was once the home of the famous physician and philosopher, Erasmus Darwin, and is now a museum dedicated to his life and work. While there are no widespread reports of paranormal activity at the house, there have been a few isolated incidents that have led some to believe that it may be haunted.

One reported ghostly sighting at Erasmus Darwin House is that of a former resident who has been seen walking through the house's halls. According to legend, the ghost is that of a former servant who died tragically while working at the house.

Another reported incident at the house involved strange noises and unexplained movements of objects. Staff members reported hearing footsteps and seeing doors opening and closing on their own, despite there being no one else in the building at the time.

Considering these reported incidents, there is lots of evidence that Erasmus Darwin House is haunted. While it is possible that the reported sightings and incidents were simply the result of overactive imaginations or natural phenomena, it's not likely.

For those who are interested in the history of the house and the life of Erasmus Darwin, a visit to the museum is still highly recommended.

Cannock Chase

Cannock Chase is a beautiful and vast area of woodland and heathland in Staffordshire, England. It is also known for its reputation as one of the most haunted locations in the UK. Cannock Chase has a long and fascinating history, dating back to prehistoric times, and this rich history has contributed to the numerous ghostly sightings reported in the area.

One of the most famous ghostly sightings at Cannock Chase is that of the "Black Eyed Child." According to legend, the Black Eyed Child is a ghostly figure with black eyes who appears to unsuspecting visitors in the woods. She is said to be a young girl who died tragically in the area and now haunts the woods, seeking to scare or harm those who encounter her.

Another famous ghostly sighting at Cannock Chase is that of a ghostly monk who has been seen walking through the woods. According to legend, he was once a member of the clergy who lived in the area and has returned as a ghost to guard the woods.

Other reported ghostly sightings at Cannock Chase include strange lights in the sky, eerie sensations, and unexplained noises.

One particularly eerie story about Cannock Chase involves a group of visitors who were exploring the woods late at night. They reported feeling a cold presence around them and hearing strange noises, including footsteps and whispers. Suddenly, one of the group members saw a ghostly figure appear before them, but when they turned around, no one was there.

The reasons for the haunting of Cannock Chase are not entirely clear, but many believe that the area's long and fascinating history, including its connections to prehistoric times, the Romans, and World War II, has contributed to the paranormal activity reported there. With its beautiful scenery and eerie atmosphere, Cannock Chase is a popular destination for history buffs and paranormal enthusiasts alike.

The Bate Hall, Macclesfield

The Bate Hall is a historic pub located in Macclesfield, Cheshire, England. It is known for its reputation as one of the most haunted pubs in the area, with numerous reports of ghostly sightings and unexplained phenomena.

One of the most famous ghostly sightings at The Bate Hall is that of a ghostly figure known as "The Lady in Grey." According to legend, she was a former landlady who died tragically and has returned to haunt the pub. Her ghost has been seen walking through the pub's halls and has been reported by visitors and staff alike.

Another reported ghostly sighting at The Bate Hall is that of a former regular who has been seen sitting at the bar, despite having passed away years earlier. Legend has it that the ghostly patron loved the pub so much that he never wanted to leave.

Other reported paranormal activity at The Bate Hall includes unexplained noises and strange movements of objects. Staff members have reported hearing footsteps, whispers, and other strange noises, even when the pub is empty. Some have also reported seeing glasses moving on their own or objects being thrown across the room.

The reasons for the haunting of The Bate Hall are not entirely clear, but many believe that the pub's long and fascinating history, including its connections to the local community and the numerous people who have lived and died in the area over the years, has contributed to the paranormal activity reported there. With its rich history and numerous ghostly sightings, The Bate Hall is a popular destination for history buffs and paranormal enthusiasts alike.

While there is no concrete evidence to suggest that The Bate Hall is truly haunted, the numerous reported ghostly sightings and unexplained phenomena make it an intriguing and potentially eerie destination. Whether you believe in ghosts or not, a visit to The Bate Hall is sure to be a memorable experience.

The Red Lion Inn, Avebury

The Red Lion Inn is a historic pub located in the village of Avebury in Wiltshire, England. It is known for its reputation as one of the most haunted pubs in the area, with numerous reports of ghostly sightings and unexplained phenomena.

One of the most famous ghostly sightings at The Red Lion Inn is that of a ghostly monk who has been seen walking through the pub's halls. According to legend, he was once a member of a local monastery and has returned as a ghost to haunt the pub.

Another reported ghostly sighting at The Red Lion Inn is that of a ghostly woman who has been seen sitting in the pub's bar. She is said to be a former landlady who died tragically and has returned to the pub to watch over it.

Other reported paranormal activity at The Red Lion Inn includes unexplained noises and strange movements of objects. Staff members have reported hearing footsteps, whispers, and other strange noises, even when the pub is empty. Some have also reported seeing glasses moving on their own or objects being thrown across the room.

One particularly spooky story about The Red Lion Inn involves a group of visitors who were exploring the pub's cellar. They reported feeling a cold presence around them and hearing strange noises, including footsteps and whispers. Suddenly, one of the group members felt a hand touch their shoulder, but when they turned around, no one was there.

In addition to these reported ghostly sightings and unexplained phenomena, The Red Lion Inn is also known for its connections to local history and legend. The pub is located in the heart of Avebury, an area known for its ancient stone circles and connections to the Druids.

The Three Tuns, Buckinghamshire

The Three Tuns is a historic pub located in the town of High Wycombe in Buckinghamshire, England. It is known for its reputation as one of the most haunted pubs in the area, with numerous reports of ghostly sightings and unexplained phenomena.

One of the most famous ghostly sightings at The Three Tuns is that of a ghostly figure known as "The Lady in Black." According to legend, she was a former landlady who died tragically and has returned to haunt the pub. Her ghost has been seen walking through the pub's halls and has been reported by visitors and staff alike.

Another reported ghostly sighting at The Three Tuns is that of a former regular who has been seen sitting at the bar, despite having passed away years earlier. Legend has it that the ghostly patron loved the pub so much that he never wanted to leave.

Other reported paranormal activity at The Three Tuns includes unexplained noises and strange movements of objects. Staff members have reported hearing footsteps, whispers, and other strange noises, even when the pub is empty. Some have also reported seeing glasses moving on their own or objects being thrown across the room.

One particularly spooky story about The Three Tuns involves a group of visitors who were exploring the pub's cellar. They reported feeling a cold presence around them and hearing strange noises, including footsteps and whispers. Suddenly, one of the group members felt a cold hand touch their shoulder, but when they turned around, no one was there.

The reasons for the haunting of The Three Tuns are not entirely clear, but many believe that the pub's long and fascinating history, including its connections to the local community and the numerous people who have lived and died in the area over the years, has contributed to the paranormal activity reported there.

Sudeley Castle, Gloucestershire

Sudeley Castle is a historic castle located in the town of Winchcombe in Gloucestershire, England. It is known for its reputation as one of the most haunted castles in the area, with numerous reports of ghostly sightings and unexplained phenomena.

One of the most famous ghostly sightings at Sudeley Castle is that of a ghostly figure known as "The Grey Lady." According to legend, she was a former resident of the castle who died tragically and has returned to haunt the castle. Her ghost has been seen walking through the castle's halls and has been reported by visitors and staff alike.

Another reported ghostly sighting at Sudeley Castle is that of a ghostly drummer boy who has been seen walking through the castle's courtyard. Legend has it that he was a former servant who was executed for a crime he did not commit and has returned as a ghost to seek revenge.

Other reported paranormal activity at Sudeley Castle includes unexplained noises and strange movements of objects. Staff members have reported hearing footsteps, whispers, and other strange noises, even when the castle is empty. Some have also reported seeing objects moving on their own or shadows moving across the walls.

One particularly spooky story about Sudeley Castle involves a group of visitors who were exploring the castle's underground tunnels. They reported feeling a cold presence around them and hearing strange noises, including footsteps and whispers. Suddenly, one of the group members felt a cold hand touch their shoulder, but when they turned around, no one was there.

The reasons for the haunting of Sudeley Castle are not entirely clear, but many believe that the castle's long and fascinating history, including its connections to royalty and the numerous people who have lived and died in the area over the years, has contributed to the paranormal activity reported there.

While there is no concrete evidence to suggest that Sudeley Castle is truly haunted, the numerous reported ghostly sightings and unexplained phenomena make it an intriguing and potentially eerie destination. Whether you believe in ghosts or not, a visit to Sudeley Castle is sure to be a memorable experience.

The Castle Keep, Newcastle upon Tyne

The Castle Keep is a historic castle located in the city of Newcastle upon Tyne, England. It is known for its reputation as one of the most haunted castles in the area, with numerous reports of ghostly sightings and unexplained phenomena. Here is everything we can find online about why The Castle Keep might be haunted:

One of the most famous ghostly sightings at The Castle Keep is that of a ghostly figure known as "The White Lady." According to legend, she was a former resident of the castle who died tragically and has returned to haunt the castle. Her ghost has been seen walking through the castle's halls and has been reported by visitors and staff alike.

Another reported ghostly sighting at The Castle Keep is that of a former prisoner who was executed in the castle's dungeons. His ghost has been seen walking through the castle's underground passages and has been reported by visitors and staff alike.

Other reported paranormal activity at The Castle Keep includes unexplained noises and strange movements of objects. Staff members have reported hearing footsteps, whispers, and other strange noises, even when the castle is empty. Some have also reported seeing objects moving on their own or shadows moving across the walls.

The Chateau Impney Hotel, Worcestershire

There are numerous reports and stories that suggest that The Chateau Impney Hotel in Worcestershire, England, may be haunted. Some of the reasons why people believe the hotel is haunted include:

Ghostly Apparitions: Several guests and staff members have reported seeing ghostly apparitions throughout the hotel. Some guests have reported seeing a woman in a white dress wandering the corridors of the hotel, while others have seen a figure in a monk's habit.

Strange Noises: Unexplained noises are a common occurrence at the Chateau Impney Hotel. Guests have reported hearing footsteps, voices, and strange banging sounds, even when there is no one else around.

Objects Moving on Their Own: Some guests have reported seeing objects moving on their own, such as doors opening and closing, and furniture shifting position.

History of the Building: The Chateau Impney Hotel is a historic building that was built in the 19th century. The building has a rich and fascinating history, which includes its use as a hospital during World War II. Many people believe that the building's history may have contributed to the paranormal activity reported there.

Previous Guests' Experiences: Many previous guests have reported paranormal experiences during their stay at the Chateau Impney Hotel. Their stories have been shared online and have contributed to the hotel's reputation as a haunted location.

Beaulieu Abbey, Hampshire

Beaulieu Abbey, located in the New Forest area of Hampshire, England, is an ancient monastery that dates back to the 13th century. Over the years, there have been numerous reports and stories of ghostly sightings and unexplained phenomena at the abbey, which has led many people to believe that it is haunted. Here are some of the reasons why people think Beaulieu Abbey is haunted:

The Abbey's History: Beaulieu Abbey has a rich and fascinating history that spans over 800 years. During this time, the abbey was home to many monks, who spent their lives in devotion to God. Over the years, the abbey has been witness to many important events, including the Dissolution of the Monasteries under Henry VIII, which resulted in the destruction of many monasteries throughout England. The abbey's long and storied history has led many to believe that it is a site of spiritual significance, and that the spirits of the monks who once lived there still linger.

Ghostly Apparitions: Many visitors to Beaulieu Abbey have reported seeing ghostly apparitions throughout the abbey's grounds. Some people have reported seeing the ghostly figure of a monk walking the halls of the abbey, while others have seen a ghostly nun wandering the grounds.

Strange Noises: Unexplained noises are a common occurrence at Beaulieu Abbey. Visitors have reported hearing footsteps, voices, and strange banging sounds, even when there is no one else around.

Objects Moving on Their Own: Some visitors have reported seeing objects moving on their own, such as doors opening and closing, and furniture shifting position.

The Abbey's Location: Beaulieu Abbey is situated in the heart of the New Forest, an area of natural beauty that is known for its spiritual significance. Many people believe that the abbey's location, combined with its history, has contributed to the paranormal activity reported there.

The Skirrid Fawr, Wales

The Skirrid Fawr, also known as the Holy Mountain, is a mountain located in Monmouthshire, Wales. It is one of the oldest mountains in Wales, and it is believed to be a place of great spiritual significance. Over the years, there have been numerous reports of paranormal activity on the mountain, which has led many people to believe that it is haunted.

One of the most common reports of paranormal activity on the Skirrid Fawr is that of ghostly apparitions. Visitors to the mountain have reported seeing ghostly figures wandering the area, including a ghostly monk who is said to haunt the mountain. Others have reported seeing strange lights and hearing unexplained noises, such as footsteps and voices.

There are also reports of a ghostly carriage that is said to travel along the mountain road at night. According to legend, the carriage is pulled by four headless horses and is driven by a headless coachman. The carriage is said to be the ghost of a local squire who was murdered on the mountain.

Another story tells of a group of Welsh warriors who were executed on the mountain by the English in the 12th century. It is said that their spirits still linger on the mountain, and that they can be seen marching across the landscape.

Perhaps the most well-known paranormal activity on the Skirrid Fawr is the alleged presence of a ghostly judge.

According to legend, the judge presided over trials on the mountain during the 17th century. He was known for his harsh and cruel sentences, and it is said that his ghost still haunts the mountain to this day. Visitors to the area have reported hearing his voice and feeling a sense of unease when in his presence.

In addition to these alleged sightings, there are numerous reports of unexplained phenomena on the mountain. Visitors have reported experiencing cold spots, feeling a sense of being watched, and seeing strange mists and orbs.

Hylton Castle, Tyne and Wear

Hylton Castle, located in Tyne and Wear, England, is an ancient castle that dates back to the 14th century. Over the years, there have been numerous reports and stories of ghostly sightings and unexplained phenomena at the castle, which has led many people to believe that it is haunted. Here are some of the reasons why people think Hylton Castle is haunted:

The Castle's History: Hylton Castle has a long and storied history, and it is said to be one of the most haunted places in the North East of England. Over the years, the castle has been witness to many important events, including battles, sieges, and even witch hunts. The castle's long and fascinating history has led many to believe that it is a site of spiritual significance, and that the spirits of those who once lived there still linger.

Ghostly Apparitions: Many visitors to Hylton Castle have reported seeing ghostly apparitions throughout the castle's grounds. Some people have reported seeing the ghostly figure of a lady in a white dress, while others have seen a ghostly soldier wandering the grounds. Some have even reported seeing a ghostly dog, which is said to be the spirit of a dog that once lived at the castle.

Strange Noises: Unexplained noises are a common occurrence at Hylton Castle. Visitors have reported hearing footsteps, voices, and strange banging sounds, even when there is no one else around.

Some people have also reported hearing the sound of battle drums, which is said to be the ghostly echo of a battle that took place at the castle centuries ago.

Cold Spots: Many visitors to Hylton Castle have reported experiencing cold spots throughout the castle's grounds. These cold spots are said to be the result of the presence of ghostly spirits, and they are often accompanied by a feeling of unease or fear.

Paranormal Activity: There have been numerous reports of paranormal activity at Hylton Castle, including objects moving on their own and the feeling of being touched by unseen hands. Some visitors have even reported feeling as though they are being watched by unseen eyes.

One of the most famous ghostly sightings at Hylton Castle is that of the Lady in White. According to legend, she is the ghost of a lady who fell in love with a soldier during the English Civil War. The soldier was killed in battle, and the lady died of a broken heart soon after. Her ghost is said to wander the castle grounds to this day, searching for her lost love.

Another famous ghostly sighting at Hylton Castle is that of the soldier. According to legend, he is the ghost of a soldier who was killed in battle at the castle during the English Civil War. His ghost is said to appear on the castle battlements, watching over the castle and its inhabitants.

St. Anne's Church, Limehouse, London

St. Anne's Church in Limehouse, London is an ancient and imposing building that has stood for centuries. It has been a place of worship for many generations of Londoners, and it is said to be one of the most haunted churches in the city. There are many reasons why people believe that St. Anne's Church is haunted, and here are some of the most compelling ones:

History: St. Anne's Church has a long and storied history, dating back to the 18th century. The church has been a focal point for the community for centuries, and it has witnessed many important events over the years. The church was bombed during the Second World War, and it has also been the site of numerous burials and funerals. All of this history has left its mark on the church, and many people believe that it is the source of the church's supernatural activity.

Ghostly Apparitions: One of the most commonly reported sightings at St. Anne's Church is that of a ghostly apparition. Visitors have reported seeing the ghost of a woman dressed in a long white gown, walking through the churchyard. Others have reported seeing the ghostly figure of a man, standing near the altar. Some people have even reported seeing ghostly children playing in the churchyard.

Unexplained Noises: Another common occurrence at St. Anne's Church is the sound of unexplained noises. Visitors have reported hearing footsteps, doors opening and closing on their own, and even the sound of whispers.

Some people have even reported hearing the sound of church bells ringing, even when no one is inside the church.

Cold Spots: Visitors to St. Anne's Church have also reported experiencing cold spots throughout the building. These cold spots are said to be the result of the presence of ghostly spirits, and they are often accompanied by a feeling of unease or fear.

Paranormal Activity: There have been numerous reports of paranormal activity at St. Anne's Church, including objects moving on their own and the feeling of being touched by unseen hands. Some visitors have even reported feeling as though they are being watched by unseen eyes.

One of the most famous ghostly sightings at St. Anne's Church is that of the White Lady. According to legend, she is the ghost of a woman who was buried in the churchyard after her husband was lost at sea. She is said to wander the churchyard, searching for her lost love.

Another famous ghostly sighting at St. Anne's Church is that of the ghostly man. According to legend, he is the ghost of a man who was killed in a duel outside the church. His ghost is said to wander the churchyard at night, searching for his opponent.

The George Hotel, Crawley

The George Hotel in Crawley, West Sussex is a historic building with a long and fascinating history. Over the years, there have been reports of supernatural activity and unexplained phenomena, leading some people to believe that the hotel is haunted.

One of the reasons people think The George Hotel is haunted is due to its connection to historic events and landmarks. The building is located near several historic battle sites, and many notable guests have stayed there over the years.

Several people have reported seeing ghostly apparitions at The George Hotel. The most commonly reported sighting is that of a ghostly figure dressed in period clothing, thought to be a former guest of the hotel. Others have reported seeing a ghostly couple holding hands, thought to be a pair of former lovers who met a tragic end.

Visitors to The George Hotel have reported hearing strange noises throughout the building, including unexplained footsteps, banging doors, and voices. Some have even reported hearing the sound of children playing in the hallways, even when there are no children staying at the hotel.

Another common occurrence at The George Hotel is the presence of cold spots. Guests have reported feeling sudden drops in temperature in certain areas of the hotel, which is believed to be the result of the presence of ghostly spirits.

Some guests have reported experiencing unexplained movements of objects in their rooms. For example, furniture has been reported to move on its own, and personal belongings have been found in different places than where they were left.

One of the most famous ghostly sightings at The George Hotel is that of a ghostly woman in white. According to legend, she is the ghost of a former guest who died in the hotel under mysterious circumstances. She is said to appear in the hotel's corridors, and guests have reported feeling a sense of dread and unease when they encounter her.

Overall, The George Hotel's reported ghostly activity has made it a popular destination for those interested in the paranormal. While there is no concrete evidence to suggest that the hotel is truly haunted, the numerous reported sightings and unexplained phenomena continue to make it a fascinating and potentially eerie location to visit.

St. Briavels Castle, Gloucestershire

St. Briavels Castle is a mediaeval castle located in Gloucestershire, England, that has a long and fascinating history. Over the years, there have been reports of supernatural activity and unexplained phenomena, leading some people to believe that the castle is haunted.

One of the reasons people think St. Briavels Castle is haunted is due to its age and history. The castle dates back to the 12th century and has been used for various purposes over the centuries, including as a royal hunting lodge, a prison, and a courthouse.

Several people have reported seeing ghostly apparitions at St. Briavels Castle. The most commonly reported sighting is that of a ghostly figure in period clothing, thought to be a former resident of the castle. Others have reported seeing a ghostly woman wandering the halls, thought to be the ghost of a former prisoner who died in the castle.

Visitors to St. Briavels Castle have reported hearing strange noises throughout the building, including unexplained footsteps, voices, and doors opening and closing. Some have even reported hearing the sound of a ghostly dog barking, even though there are no dogs on the premises.

Another common occurrence at St. Briavels Castle is the presence of cold spots.

Guests have reported feeling sudden drops in temperature in certain areas of the castle, which is believed to be the result of the presence of ghostly spirits.

Some guests have reported experiencing unexplained movements of objects in their rooms. For example, furniture has been reported to move on its own, and personal belongings have been found in different places than where they were left.

One of the most famous ghostly sightings at St. Briavels Castle is that of a ghostly drummer. According to legend, the drummer was killed during a battle that took place near the castle and his ghost has been heard drumming his drum in the castle courtyard. Some guests have reported hearing the drumming late at night, and feeling a sense of unease when they encounter the ghostly presence.

Overall, St. Briavels Castle's reported ghostly activity has made it a popular destination for those interested in the paranormal. While there is no concrete evidence to suggest that the castle is truly haunted, the numerous reported sightings and unexplained phenomena continue to make it a fascinating and potentially eerie location to visit.

The Golden Fleece, York

The Golden Fleece is a pub located in York, England, that has a long and storied history. Over the years, there have been numerous reports of supernatural activity and unexplained phenomena, leading many to believe that the pub is haunted.

One of the reasons people think The Golden Fleece is haunted is because of its age. The pub dates back to the early 1500s and has been used for various purposes over the centuries, including as a brothel and a courthouse. It is believed that the building was also used as a holding cell for prisoners, which may have contributed to the reported paranormal activity.

Several people have reported seeing ghostly apparitions at The Golden Fleece. The most commonly reported sighting is that of a ghostly figure of a young girl who is believed to have been murdered on the premises. Others have reported seeing a ghostly figure of a man in a bowler hat, thought to be the ghost of a former landlord of the pub.

Visitors to The Golden Fleece have reported hearing strange noises throughout the building, including unexplained footsteps, voices, and doors opening and closing. Some have even reported feeling a ghostly presence or a sense of being watched.

Another common occurrence at The Golden Fleece is the presence of cold spots. Guests have reported feeling sudden drops in temperature in certain areas of the pub, which is believed to be the result of the presence of ghostly spirits.

Some guests have reported experiencing unexplained movements of objects in their rooms. For example, items have been reported to move on their own, and personal belongings have been found in different places than where they were left.

One of the most famous ghostly sightings at The Golden Fleece is that of a ghostly figure of a woman in black who is said to haunt Room 4. According to legend, the woman was a former landlady of the pub who was murdered by her husband. Guests have reported seeing the ghostly figure of the woman and feeling a sense of unease when they enter the room.

The Olde Bell, Hurley, Berkshire

The Olde Bell in Hurley, Berkshire is a historic hotel that dates back to the 12th century. Over the years, the hotel has been the site of numerous reports of supernatural activity, leading many to believe that it is haunted.

One of the reasons people think The Olde Bell is haunted is because of its age. The hotel has been in operation for over 800 years, and has served as a coaching inn, a farm, and a private residence. It is believed that the building's long history has contributed to the reports of paranormal activity.

Many guests have reported seeing ghostly apparitions at The Olde Bell. The most commonly reported sighting is that of a ghostly figure of a monk. The monk is believed to be the ghost of a former resident of the building, who was a member of a religious order that once occupied the site.

Other guests have reported hearing unexplained noises throughout the building, including footsteps, doors opening and closing, and mysterious voices. Some have even reported feeling a ghostly presence or a sense of being watched.

One of the most famous ghostly sightings at The Olde Bell is that of a ghostly figure of a woman in white who is said to haunt the dining room. According to legend, the woman was a former resident of the building who died tragically, and her ghost continues to wander the premises.

Oxford Castle, Oxfordshire

Oxford Castle, located in the heart of Oxford, is a popular tourist destination and historical site. The castle, which dates back to the 11th century, has a long and complex history that has led many to believe that it is haunted by the spirits of those who once inhabited it.

One of the main reasons people believe Oxford Castle is haunted is due to its violent past. The castle was originally built by the Normans, and was used as a prison for many years. During this time, it was the site of numerous executions, including the execution of the famous Scottish patriot William Wallace in 1305.

Visitors to Oxford Castle have reported hearing strange noises, such as footsteps and the sound of rattling chains, as well as feeling sudden changes in temperature. Some have even reported seeing ghostly apparitions of former prisoners and execution victims.

One of the most commonly reported sightings at Oxford Castle is that of a ghostly woman in white. According to legend, the woman was a former prisoner who was executed for a crime she did not commit. Her ghost is said to wander the castle, seeking justice for her wrongful conviction and execution.

Another ghostly presence reported at Oxford Castle is that of a former executioner. Visitors have reported feeling a sudden chill or a feeling of unease when passing by the execution chamber, which is believed to be the site of the executioner's ghostly presence.

In addition to these sightings, visitors have reported other paranormal phenomena, such as unexplained smells and the feeling of being touched by an unseen presence. Some have even reported hearing voices and seeing strange shadows moving across the walls.

Overall, the reported hauntings at Oxford Castle continue to fascinate and intrigue visitors from around the world. While there is no concrete evidence to prove the existence of ghosts, the castle's dark and bloody history has led many to believe that it is home to the spirits of the dead.

The White Hart Hotel, Harrogate

The White Hart Hotel in Harrogate, North Yorkshire, is a historic hotel that dates back to the 18th century. Over the years, it has gained a reputation as one of the most haunted hotels in the UK, with many guests reporting strange occurrences and paranormal activity.

One of the main reasons people believe The White Hart Hotel is haunted is due to its history. The hotel is built on the site of an old workhouse, which is said to have been a place of great suffering and despair. It is also believed to have been a site of public execution in the past.

Guests at The White Hart Hotel have reported hearing strange noises and experiencing unexplained phenomena, such as doors opening and closing by themselves and objects moving on their own. Some have even reported seeing ghostly apparitions, including a lady in a long white dress and a spectral figure believed to be a former stablehand.

One of the most commonly reported sightings at The White Hart Hotel is that of a ghostly maid who is said to have hanged herself in one of the rooms. Guests have reported seeing her ghostly figure walking the corridors, and some have even reported feeling her presence in their rooms.

Other reported hauntings at The White Hart Hotel include the sound of ghostly footsteps and a mysterious presence that is said to haunt the hotel's cellar. Some guests have also reported feeling a sudden drop in temperature, or the feeling of being touched by an unseen presence.

Despite the reported hauntings, The White Hart Hotel remains a popular destination for visitors from all over the world. Whether or not the hotel is truly haunted remains a matter of debate, but its reputation as one of the UK's most haunted hotels continues to attract those with an interest in the paranormal.

Coombe Abbey, Warwickshire

Coombe Abbey is a beautiful historic country house in Warwickshire, England. It was originally founded as a monastery in the 12th century before being converted into a grand residence in the 16th century. The Abbey has a rich history and has had a variety of inhabitants over the years, which has led many to believe that it is haunted.

One of the main reasons people believe Coombe Abbey is haunted is because of the many reports of paranormal activity that have been made by visitors and staff over the years. There have been numerous reports of strange noises, including footsteps, voices, and the sound of doors opening and closing on their own. Some people have even reported seeing ghostly apparitions, including a spectral figure known as the "White Lady."

The White Lady is said to be the ghost of a former resident of Coombe Abbey, who was betrayed by her lover and murdered. Her ghostly figure has been spotted in various parts of the Abbey, and some people have reported feeling a sudden drop in temperature when she is near.

Other reported hauntings at Coombe Abbey include the ghostly apparition of a monk, believed to be one of the former inhabitants of the original monastery. The ghost of a former stable boy has also been reported, as well as the spirit of a young girl who is said to haunt the library.

The Black Horse, Pluckley

The Black Horse pub in Pluckley, Kent, is reputed to be one of the most haunted pubs in the UK. The village of Pluckley itself has a reputation for being haunted, with many ghostly sightings and paranormal occurrences reported over the years. The Black Horse is said to be particularly haunted, with a number of reported sightings and unexplained occurrences.

One of the reasons people believe The Black Horse is haunted is because of the age of the building. It is believed to date back to the 14th century and has had many different uses over the years, including a coaching inn and a smuggler's hideout. This long history has led many to believe that the pub is haunted by the ghosts of former residents and visitors.

There have been numerous reports of ghostly sightings and unexplained activity at The Black Horse. Visitors have reported seeing ghostly apparitions, including the ghost of a former landlord who is said to haunt the pub's cellar. Others have reported hearing strange noises and seeing objects move on their own.

One of the most commonly reported hauntings at The Black Horse is that of a young girl who is said to have died in a fire at the pub many years ago. Her ghostly figure has been seen by many visitors, often in the upstairs rooms of the pub. Some people have also reported feeling a sudden drop in temperature or feeling an unexplained presence when she is near.

Despite the reported hauntings, The Black Horse remains a popular destination for visitors and locals alike. The current owners of the pub have embraced its haunted history and have even introduced a ghost tour for those brave enough to explore its spooky past.

The Grand Theatre, Wolverhampton

The Grand Theatre in Wolverhampton, England, is a beautiful historic building that has been entertaining audiences for over a century. However, over the years, many people have reported strange occurrences and ghostly sightings, leading some to believe that the theatre is haunted.

One of the main reasons people believe The Grand Theatre is haunted is because of its age. It was built in 1894 and has had a long and varied history, including hosting many famous performers over the years. This rich history has led many to believe that the theatre is home to a number of ghosts and spirits.

There have been numerous reports of ghostly sightings and unexplained occurrences at The Grand Theatre. Some people have reported seeing ghostly apparitions, including the ghost of a former actress who is said to haunt the dressing rooms. Others have reported hearing strange noises and unexplained voices, as well as feeling sudden drops in temperature or unexplained cold spots.

One of the most famous ghostly sightings at The Grand Theatre is that of a former stagehand who is said to have died in the theatre many years ago. His ghostly figure has been spotted by many visitors and staff, often in the backstage areas of the theatre. Some people have also reported feeling an unexplained presence or seeing objects move on their own.

Rosslyn Chapel, Midlothian, Scotland

Rosslyn Chapel, located in Midlothian, Scotland, is a beautiful and historic chapel that has been the subject of many legends and tales of paranormal activity. Many people believe that the chapel is haunted, and there have been numerous reports of ghostly sightings and unexplained phenomena over the years.

One of the reasons people believe Rosslyn Chapel is haunted is because of its long and mysterious history. The chapel was built in the 15th century and is filled with intricate carvings and symbols that have been the subject of much speculation and mystery. Some people believe that these carvings are linked to the Knights Templar, and that the chapel holds many secrets and hidden meanings.

There have been numerous reports of ghostly sightings and unexplained activity at Rosslyn Chapel. Some visitors have reported seeing ghostly apparitions, including the ghost of a monk who is said to haunt the chapel's crypt. Others have reported hearing strange noises and unexplained voices, as well as feeling sudden drops in temperature or unexplained cold spots.

One of the most famous ghostly sightings at Rosslyn Chapel is that of a "phantom drummer". This ghostly figure is said to be the ghost of a man who was buried alive within the walls of the chapel. Visitors have reported hearing the sound of a drum being played, as well as feeling an unexplained presence or seeing shadowy figures in the chapel's corridors.

Despite the reported hauntings, Rosslyn Chapel remains a popular destination for visitors from all over the world. The chapel's mysterious and intriguing history continues to fascinate people, and its haunting tales only add to its allure.

The Globe Inn, Dumfries, Scotland

The Globe Inn, located in Dumfries, Scotland, is a historic and charming establishment that has been around for over 200 years. However, it is not just its rich history that draws people to The Globe Inn. Many people believe that the inn is haunted by ghosts, and there have been numerous reports of ghostly sightings and unexplained phenomena over the years. In this blog post, we will explore the reasons behind these ghostly tales and try to separate fact from fiction.

One of the main reasons people believe The Globe Inn is haunted is because of its long and interesting history. The inn was established in the 1700s and quickly became a popular destination for travellers and locals alike. Over the years, it has hosted many famous guests, including Robert Burns, who is said to have penned some of his most famous works while staying at The Globe Inn.

There have been many reports of ghostly activity at The Globe Inn over the years. Visitors have reported seeing ghostly apparitions, hearing strange noises, and feeling unexplained cold spots or drops in temperature. Many of these sightings have been attributed to the ghost of a woman known as "Annie Laurie", who is said to haunt the inn to this day.

According to legend, Annie Laurie was a beautiful young woman who fell in love with a soldier. However, her father did not approve of the relationship and arranged for her to marry another man. Annie was heartbroken and is said to have died of a broken heart. Her ghost is said to haunt The Globe Inn, and many visitors have reported seeing her apparition or feeling her presence in the inn's rooms and corridors.

Another famous ghostly sighting at The Globe Inn is that of a young boy. The ghostly boy is said to haunt the inn's cellar, and visitors have reported hearing his laughter or seeing his apparition in the dimly lit cellar. It is not clear who the boy was or why he haunts the inn, but his ghostly presence has been reported by many over the years.

The Old Bell Hotel, Malmesbury

The Old Bell Hotel, located in Malmesbury, Wiltshire, is a historic hotel that dates back to the 13th century. Over the years, the hotel has played host to many famous guests, including King Charles II and Sir Winston Churchill. However, the hotel's rich history is not the only reason people are drawn to it. Many people believe that The Old Bell Hotel is also home to a number of spirits and ghosts. In this blog post, we will explore the reasons behind these ghostly tales and try to separate fact from fiction.

One of the reasons people believe The Old Bell Hotel is haunted is because of its long and fascinating history. The hotel has been in operation for over 800 years and has seen many changes over the centuries. It is said that some of the spirits that haunt the hotel are former residents or guests who never left.

One of the most famous ghosts associated with The Old Bell Hotel is a woman known as the "Grey Lady". According to legend, the Grey Lady was a former resident of the hotel who was killed in a fire. Her ghost is said to haunt the hotel's corridors and rooms, and many guests have reported seeing her apparition or feeling her presence.

Another famous ghostly tale associated with The Old Bell Hotel is that of a young girl who is said to haunt the hotel's garden. It is said that the girl drowned in a nearby river and her ghost now wanders the garden, searching for her lost doll.

Many guests have reported other strange occurrences at the hotel, such as unexplained noises, doors opening and closing on their own, and objects moving inexplicably. Some people believe that these occurrences are caused by the spirits that are said to haunt the hotel.

The Rose and Crown Hotel, Colchester

The Rose and Crown Hotel is a historic hotel located in Colchester, Essex, which dates back to the 14th century. The hotel has a rich and storied history, having hosted many notable guests over the years. However, along with its fascinating history, the hotel is also known for being a hotspot for paranormal activity. Many guests and staff members have reported strange and unexplainable occurrences, leading some to believe that the hotel is haunted by malevolent spirits.

One of the most commonly reported paranormal incidents at The Rose and Crown Hotel is the sensation of being touched or pushed by an unseen force. Many guests have reported feeling an invisible hand on their shoulder or back, while others have reported being pushed or tripped by an unseen presence. Some people have even reported feeling as though they were being choked or strangled by an invisible entity.

Another eerie occurrence at The Rose and Crown Hotel is the sound of unexplained footsteps and voices. Many guests have reported hearing footsteps coming from empty hallways, and some have even heard whispers and disembodied voices. The hotel staff has also reported hearing strange noises and voices when no one else is around.

Perhaps the most frightening experience that guests have reported at The Rose and Crown Hotel is the sighting of apparitions. Many people have claimed to see ghostly figures wandering the hotel's corridors and rooms, and some have reported being visited by malevolent spirits in their sleep.

While the exact cause of the paranormal activity at The Rose and Crown Hotel is unknown, many people believe that the hotel's history is to blame. The building has been in operation for over 600 years and has seen many changes over the centuries, including being used as a courthouse and a prison. Some people believe that the energy of those who were once held captive or punished within the hotel's walls may be responsible for the reported hauntings.

East Riddlesden Hall, West Yorkshire

East Riddlesden Hall is a 17th-century manor house located in Keighley, West Yorkshire. While the house is now a popular tourist attraction, it is also well-known for its reputation as a haunted location. Many people believe that the house is home to a variety of ghosts and spirits, and there have been numerous reports of paranormal activity at the site.

One of the most commonly reported incidents at East Riddlesden Hall is the sighting of apparitions. Visitors have reported seeing ghostly figures wandering the halls and rooms of the house, with some describing the ghosts as being dressed in clothing from the 17th century. Some people have even claimed to see the apparitions disappear before their eyes.
Another common occurrence at East Riddlesden Hall is the sound of unexplained noises.

Visitors have reported hearing footsteps, voices, and strange knocking sounds when no one else is around. Some people have also reported feeling sudden drops in temperature, or feeling as though they are being watched by an unseen presence.

One particularly eerie room at East Riddlesden Hall is the kitchen. The room is said to be haunted by the ghost of a woman who was once a servant in the house. Visitors have reported seeing the ghostly figure of a woman dressed in a long skirt and apron, who seems to be going about her daily tasks as if she is still alive.

There are also reports of a ghostly presence in the upstairs bedrooms of the house. Visitors have reported feeling as though someone is watching them or touching them while they sleep, and some have even claimed to have seen the ghostly figure of a man standing at the foot of their bed.

So why do so many people believe that East Riddlesden Hall is haunted? One theory is that the site's long history is to blame. The house has been in existence for over 400 years and has seen many different owners and inhabitants over the centuries. Some people believe that the energy of these past residents may still be lingering in the house, leading to the reported hauntings.

Whatever the cause of the reported paranormal activity, there is no denying that East Riddlesden Hall is a fascinating and eerie location. Whether you are a believer in the paranormal or not, a visit to this haunted house is sure to be an unforgettable experience.

The Leper Chapel, Cambridge

The Leper Chapel, also known as the Chapel of St. Mary Magdalene, is located in Cambridge, England. The chapel was built in the 12th century and was originally used to provide religious services for the local leper community. Today, the chapel is a popular tourist attraction and a venue for events such as concerts and exhibitions. However, many people believe that the chapel is haunted by spirits from its dark and turbulent past.

One of the most commonly reported paranormal experiences at the Leper Chapel is the sighting of ghostly figures. Visitors have reported seeing apparitions of monks and nuns wandering the halls and grounds of the chapel. Some have even claimed to see the ghostly figure of a leper walking through the chapel, wearing tattered clothing and bearing the telltale marks of the disease.

Another common experience reported by visitors to the Leper Chapel is the feeling of being watched or followed. Many people have reported feeling a cold, eerie presence when visiting the chapel, as if someone is standing right behind them. Some have even claimed to have been touched or pushed by an unseen force.

There are also reports of unexplained sounds and noises at the Leper Chapel. Visitors have reported hearing footsteps, whispers, and even chanting coming from the chapel, even when no one else is around. Some people have also reported feeling as though they are being surrounded by a palpable energy, as if the chapel is alive with supernatural activity.

So why do so many people believe that the Leper Chapel is haunted? One theory is that the chapel's long and storied history is to blame. The chapel has seen many different uses and inhabitants over the centuries, from a religious sanctuary for lepers to a hospital during times of war. It is believed that the energy of these past events may still be present in the chapel, leading to the reported hauntings.

Another theory is that the chapel's location on the edge of town, surrounded by fields and countryside, may contribute to its ghostly reputation. In the quiet and isolated setting, it is easy to imagine that the chapel is a haven for spirits and ghosts.

The Brookside Theatre, Romford

The Brookside Theatre, located in the town of Romford, East London, has long been considered one of the most haunted theatres in the UK. Opened in 2012, it has quickly gained a reputation for ghostly occurrences and strange happenings. There have been many reported sightings of apparitions and strange noises, leading many to believe that the theatre is home to a number of restless spirits.

One of the most commonly reported ghosts at the Brookside Theatre is that of a former performer. It is said that this ghostly figure can be seen on stage and in the wings, dressed in a white costume. Many people have reported feeling a strange presence while watching performances, and some have even claimed to have seen this ghostly figure sitting in the audience.

In addition to the performer ghost, there have been reports of other spectral entities inhabiting the theatre. Some people have reported hearing disembodied voices, while others have claimed to have felt an icy breath on their necks. One common report is that of doors opening and closing on their own, and lights flickering for no apparent reason.

There are a number of theories as to why the Brookside Theatre may be haunted. Some believe that it is due to the theatre's location, which is said to be on top of an old burial ground. Others believe that it is due to the fact that the theatre was built on the site of an old hospital, and that the spirits of those who passed away there are still lingering in the building.

Despite the many reports of ghostly activity, the owners of the Brookside Theatre have embraced their haunted reputation. They even offer ghost tours to visitors, which take them around the theatre and highlight some of the most famous ghostly occurrences. Whether you believe in ghosts or not, the Brookside Theatre is certainly an intriguing place to visit for those interested in the paranormal.

Conclusion

In conclusion, Haunted Britain The Paranormal Tourist's UK Handbook is a comprehensive guide for those interested in exploring the haunted history of the United Kingdom. From castles to pubs, cemeteries to theatres, this guide offers a diverse range of locations for ghost hunters to visit and investigate.

The stories behind these haunted locations are fascinating and often steeped in history, adding an extra layer of intrigue to any paranormal investigation. The guide provides detailed information about each location, including its history, reported hauntings, and any previous paranormal investigations.

While some may be sceptical about the existence of ghosts, the popularity of paranormal tourism shows that there is a significant interest in the unexplained. The UK has a rich and varied history, and the ghosts that are said to haunt its buildings and landscapes are a part of that history. Whether you are a seasoned ghost hunter or just curious about the paranormal, Haunted Britain The Paranormal Tourist's UK Handbook is an invaluable resource for exploring the haunted side of the UK.

More books by this author:

- Haunted Cannock Chase
- Ghosts of Cannock Chase
- Leave This House
- On the hunt for the British Bigfoot
- Skinwalkers
- In Love with a Ghost
- UFOs, Werewolves & the Pigman
- Scary but True: Ghost stories from around the world
- Thr Black-Eyed Child of Cannock Chase

Get them all from Amazon. Just search "Lee Brickley" or the title you require.

Thank you for buying this book. Have a spooky time exploring the UK!